A GUIDE TO
INTERPRETING SCRIPTURE

A Guide to Interpreting Scripture

Michael Kyomya

ZONDERVAN®

ZONDERVAN

A Guide to Interpreting Scripture
Copyright © 2010 by Michael Kyomya

Michael Kyomya has asserted his right under the Copyright, Designs, and Patents Act 1988 to be identified as Author of this Work

Original edition © 2008 by HippoBooks

This edition of *A Guide to Interpreting Scripture* is published by arrangement with Langham Publishing

ISBN 978-0-310-10704-0 (softcover)

Requests for information should be addressed to:
Zondervan, *3900 Sparks Dr. SE, Grand Rapids, Michigan 49546*

Cover design: projectluz.mac.com
Book design: To a Tee Ltd, www.2at.com

Printed in the United States of America

19 20 21 22 23 24 /LSC/ 15 14 13 12 11 10 9 8 7 6 5 4 3 2 1

Dedication

To my dear wife, Florence, and our children, Eve, Martha, Timothy, Christa and Mervyn as well as to our daughter-in-law, Salome, son-in-law, Clifton, and our grandchildren, Michael, Martha and Suubi

CONTENTS

FOREWORD

If you are reading this, I assume you are trying to understand what I am saying. That intuitive process, which we often take for granted, is called interpretation. It is needed each time we read the Bible.

The Bible is a complex book. It comes from cultures thousands of years removed from ours, and the production spanned many centuries and many authors. Moreover, each book has two authors – God and the human author. Therefore, the Bible is not like any other book, and reading and understanding it is not quite like reading any other book. Because the Bible is a divine work, it is very important to understand its message so that we can apply it properly. Thus this *Guide to Interpreting Scripture* offers an important service by helping us to read the Bible well.

Because the Bible is special, we sometimes attempt to read it in ways we would not read any other book, looking for hidden meanings or twists of meaning. There is a danger that we may think that God is saying something to us by these special means when he may not be speaking at all. Sorting out how God speaks to us through his word is one of the most important things people can do.

In Africa, where Christianity is growing and all kinds of teaching abound, teachers and Bible students must know how to sift through information that is presented as biblical to find what truly is biblical. The book you hold in your hand presents a simple, but not simplistic, approach to doing this. Dr. Kyomya stresses the importance of appreciating the context of Scripture and its unity and the need to apply Scripture. He also alerts us to ways in which we can miss what the Bible offers us.

Dr. Kyomya expertly opens up how to read the Bible with an eye to finding its message, not creating one of our own, and thus it is a joy to commend this book to you. I am confident that if you put the principles outlined here into practice, you will be able to interpret Scripture with the care and respect that God's word requires. May the Lord bless your study of his word and your preparation to understand what God says to his people through it.

Darrell L. Bock
Dallas, Texas
September 2, 2009

PREFACE

Every believer needs to read the Bible. We learned this in Sunday school when we sang:

> Read your Bible, pray every day, pray every day, pray every day!
> Read your Bible, pray every day, if you want to grow!

This reminder is good. As God's people, Christians need to read the Bible. They really do. But Christians need more than just exhortation to read the Bible; they also need to be empowered to do so profitably. They need to know how to correctly handle the word of truth (2 Tim 2:15). Those few who seek training in Bible colleges and seminaries will gain training in interpretation, but sadly the vast majority of Christians never have any training at all in this area. This was brought home to me after a seminar where I spoke about Acts 17:10–11:

> As soon as it was night, the believers sent Paul and Silas away to Berea. On arriving there, they went to the Jewish synagogue. Now the Berean Jews were of more noble character than those in Thessalonica, for they received the message with great eagerness and examined the Scriptures every day to see if what Paul said was true.

I urged the people to guard against false teaching. I exhorted them to read the Bible themselves and not accept whatever someone like a teacher or preacher says. I pointed them to the example of the believers in Berea, who listened to the Apostle Paul preach and teach, and then went back to check what the Bible had to say for themselves. The Bereans wanted to find out whether what Paul had said was really in the Bible.

Afterwards, a young woman who had attended the seminar came up to me: "It's all very well to tell us to be like the believers at Berea and read the Bible ourselves – but we need some help, some empowerment, so that we can rightly handle the word of truth." Her words hit home.

The same thought was echoed at another forum. At a board meeting of the Bible Society of Uganda, the general secretary reported that the international body of which we were part, the United Bible Societies, had decided that it would not only sell Bibles but also work to empower people to read the Bible.

I became convinced of the need for believers, ministers of the word and ministerial agencies to share the burden of empowering people to read the Bible. This work is especially urgent in light of the many dangerous cults that have sprung up and the widespread but unwholesome reading and teaching of God's word.

With all these factors in mind, I decided to write this book to contribute a resource that will (I hope) empower many people to read the Bible and read it wholesomely. Interpretation is a technical subject, but I have written this book in an enjoyable and easy-to-read style so that many people can read it and at least become aware of the fundamentals of interpretation. Those who have some training in this subject will find the book a handy summary of the basics for their refreshment.

I pray that God will use *A Guide to Interpreting Scripture* for his glory and the good of his church, even beyond my expectations (Eph 3:20).

ACKNOWLEDGEMENTS

The first person who must be acknowledged is my wife, Florence, who has lovingly encouraged me over the years and repeatedly reminded me to write. She is a precious blessing in my life and calling. I also thank our children for their enthusiasm and encouragement as I worked on this book and for proofreading the manuscript.

Particular thanks go to Timothy Kyomya, with whom we worked very closely in the proofreading and editing. Persis Wakabi typed the whole manuscript, and I am truly appreciative. Dr. Darrell Bock, my professor at Dallas Theological Seminary, also helped and encouraged me in the process of publishing this book and has kindly written the foreword.

Isobel Stevenson and Debbie Head, the editors, have provided much encouragement and excellent guidance. I am truly grateful. Any shortcomings in the book remain entirely my responsibility. I also thank the HippoBooks publishing consortium (WordAlive in Kenya, ACTS in Nigeria and Step in Ghana) for kindly taking on this project together with Zondervan.

To God, who alone makes all things possible, be all the glory.

ABBREVIATIONS

ESV English Standard Version
KJV King James Version
NASB New American Standard Bible
NET New English Translation
NIV New International Version
NKJV New King James Version
NRSV New Revised Standard Version
RSV Revised Standard Version
TEV Today's English Version / Good News Bible

1

INTRODUCTION

A preacher once said, "I am not bothered by the various interpretations of this Bible passage. I only care about what the Bible says." Like that preacher, many people think that interpretation is simply an academic exercise that can be divorced from what the Bible actually says. This is a misconception. We cannot know what the Bible says without interpreting it.

Lack of interpretation in reading the Bible can cause severe problems, which have led many people astray. For example, how do we interpret the title "Son of God" ascribed to Jesus in the Gospel of John? Some groups teach that since Jesus is the "Son" of God, he must be less than God. They fail to recognize that the gospel writer is using the word "son" in a different way from the way it is used today.

Even some well-meaning preachers and teachers have stumbled and misled others because of their lack of interpretation. They preach exhilarating sermons that are interpretatively wanting and hollow. I remember one such sermon. An influential preacher was preaching on Genesis 13:10 in which Lot chose the "low" lands of Sodom and Gomorrah after Abraham gave him a choice of where to live. This preacher made much of the term "low" lands. To my consternation he said that "low" in the Bible connotes evil. Thus low land is evil, while high land is good. According to the preacher, this was why Lot's choice proved to be calamitous.

Many in the audience were very impressed by this unique interpretation, but unfortunately it was rooted only in the preacher's fertile imagination. There was no evidence from the Bible to back him up. Clearly, the plain or "low" land was not evil because it was low but because the people living there were evil and ungodly. After all, Abraham, Isaac and Jacob lived in the low valley of Hebron, and it was fine (Gen 13:18; 35:27; 37:14).

Flawed interpretations of the Bible are widespread in the church. That is why it is so important that we learn how to interpret the Bible. We do well to remember what our Lord said about the Sadducees who did not believe in the resurrection:

> You are in error because you do not know the Scriptures or the power of God. At the resurrection people will neither marry nor be given in marriage; they will be like the angels in heaven. But about the resurrection of the dead – have you not read what God said to you, 'I am the God of Abraham, the God of Isaac, and the God of Jacob'? He is not the God of the dead but of the living. (Matt 22:29–32).

The Sadducees knew the verse that Jesus quoted. They had read it before, but they did not know its interpretation and they went astray.

When Paul talks of the tragedy of the Jews' rejection of Jesus, he says:

> Brothers and sisters, my heart's desire and prayer to God for the Israelites is that they may be saved. For I can testify about them that they are zealous for God, but their zeal is *not based on knowledge*. Since they did not know the righteousness of God and sought to establish their own, they did not submit to God's righteousness. (Rom 10:1–3)

This whole tragedy had bad interpretation at its core.

We should also remember Paul's exhortation to Timothy: "Do your best to present yourself to God as one approved, a worker who does not need to be ashamed and who correctly handles the word of truth" (2 Tim 2:15).

Today, many people show great zeal for God and zealously preach and teach the word of God, but lack skill in interpretation. It behoves us to pay close attention to this issue because "then we will no longer be infants, tossed back and forth by the waves, and blown here and there by every wind of teaching" (Eph 4:14). We should be like the people of Berea in the book of Acts, who were commended because they were "of more noble character than those in Thessalonica, for they received the message with great eagerness and examined the Scriptures every day to see if what Paul said was true" (Acts 17:11).

It is interesting to note whose teaching the people of Berea were checking: It was that of the great Apostle Paul! He was teaching and preaching to them, and they were checking whether his message concurred with the word of God. We need to be Bereans today and check all the preaching and teaching we hear, whether it comes from an eloquent and famous preacher or an acclaimed scholar or teacher. We need to be on our guard and to make sure that what they say concurs with the Scriptures. To be able to do this we need to know how to interpret the Scriptures correctly. This applies to all of us – preachers and teachers, students of the Bible and ordinary believers. We all urgently need to learn more about interpretation.

Some years back, some groups disdained biblical and theological training, scholars and theologians. I am happy that such thinking is becoming more and more a thing of the past, because the concept of training is not of the devil; it is of God. Rather than reject all of scholarship, we need to distinguish between good and bad scholarship. God has used, and continues to use, good scholarship and theology to promote the gospel. Remember, even the Bible translation you use is a product of hard work by scholars and theologians.

Anyone who disparages teaching or training has no right to be teaching and training others. If you are teaching others, why should you not be taught and trained? Proverbs 12:15 reminds us that even "the wise listen to advice". Mark 4:34 says that the apostles were trained and taught: When Jesus "was alone with his own disciples, he explained everything" to them. Jesus could have breathed all knowledge into his disciples, but he chose to train and teach them for three years.

Training in the Bible and theology is crucial because without it church growth will be stunted and the church will go astray. And training in how to interpret the Bible is vital because all preaching depends on interpretation, all teaching depends on interpretation, all theology depends on interpretation. The rapid growth and mushrooming of churches in many parts of the world creates a crying need for trained leaders who will be able to nurture them.

This book deals with the need for interpretation, the definition of interpretation, the foundation of interpretation, approaches to interpretation, some principles of interpretation, and some hindrances in interpretation. It also considers the matter of application, which is the logical and necessary step after interpretation.

The three appendices deal with a few specific issues. The first looks at the interpretation of Wisdom literature such as the books of Proverbs and Psalms. The second deals with interpreting figures of speech, and the final one lists additional resources that can help you to interpret Scripture.

2

NEED FOR INTERPRETATION

One day, my wife and I were with our friend Jane when she heard that someone called John had just died. Jane responded, "Oh, that's wonderful!" I wondered what was going on.

Later, I commented to my wife, "Jane must really have hated John!"

"No. She loved him very much," my wife replied.

I persisted, "But when she was told that John was dead, she said, 'That's wonderful'."

"Oh," said my wife, "Jane doesn't know much English. And in her part of the world, 'wonderful' usually means 'bad – very bad'."

I replied, "That's wonderful!"

Simple Misunderstandings

Sometimes we misunderstand what a person says or writes and we need help to interpret what they meant. An example of this is found in the Bible. Just after Jesus had told Peter to follow him, Peter asked Jesus about John, saying, "Lord, what about him?" Jesus answered:

> "If I want him to remain alive until I return, what is that to you? You must follow me." However, the disciples misunderstood what Jesus said: Because of this, the rumour spread among the

believers that this disciple would not die. But Jesus did not say
that he would not die; he only said, "If I want him to remain
alive until I return, what is that to you?" (John 21:21–23)

The disciples missed the point and needed help with their
interpretation.

The Corinthians also misunderstood Paul's instructions. Paul had
written them a letter telling them not to associate with people who were
"immoral". However, the Corinthians mistakenly thought that Paul had
told them not to associate with immoral people in general. So when he
wrote to them again, Paul said,

> I wrote to you in my letter not to associate with the immoral
> people – not at all meaning the people of this world who are
> immoral, or the greedy and swindlers, or idolaters. In that case
> you would have to leave this world. (1 Cor 5:9–10 RSV)

Paul was writing to the Corinthians in their own language – the language
they knew very well. But they still misunderstood him! This goes to
show how easy it is to stumble even over what is familiar to us.

To give another example, not long after feeding four thousand
people with only seven loaves of bread, Jesus and his disciples prepared
to cross the Sea of Galilee (Mark 8:11–21). Just before their departure
the Pharisees argued with Jesus and demanded he give them a sign from
heaven. Then as they set out in the boat, the disciples discovered that
they had forgotten to bring bread with them. All they had was one
loaf.

As they were sailing along, Jesus charged them, "Be careful ... Watch
out for the yeast of the Pharisees and that of Herod." Yeast is used
in bread-making, and, as you can imagine, bread was the "familiar"
and consuming topic of conversation at that moment. "They discussed
this with one another and said, 'It is because we have no bread.'" The
disciples took the familiar meaning, or the meaning that quickly came to
their minds, and betrayed their lack of trust in Jesus' power to provide
abundantly, even from a little.

This interpretation brought a stinging rebuke from Jesus. He had
just demonstrated his power to perform miracles and provide food by

abundantly feeding four thousand people with only seven loaves, and on an earlier occasion he had fed more than five thousand with only five loaves. Knowing all this, the disciples still worried about not having enough bread? So Jesus asked them, "Do you still not understand?"

The disciples took the familiar meaning of the word "yeast", the meaning that quickly came to their minds. But they were mistaken.

Learning skills in interpretation will sensitize you to move more cautiously and will minimize such stumbles.

Sometimes we misunderstand what someone says or what the Bible says, even when the words are familiar.

Difficult Passages

The Bible contains some passages that are difficult to understand. Peter acknowledged this when he said:

> Bear in mind that our Lord's patience means salvation, just as our dear brother Paul also wrote you with the wisdom that God gave him. He writes the same way in all his letters, speaking in them of these matters. His letters contain some things that are hard to understand. (2 Pet 3:15–16a)

This is the Apostle Peter pointing this out! If he acknowledged that some passages are difficult, then surely we too should move cautiously and learn interpretation. If we do not, we may stumble over the difficult passages that, Peter continues, "ignorant and unstable people distort, as they do the other Scriptures, to their own destruction" (2 Pet 3:16b).

Different Contexts

If some of the disciples could misunderstand Jesus when he spoke to them face to face, if the early church could misunderstand Paul's words in his letter, and if Peter acknowledged that some things in Paul's letters were difficult to understand, we can certainly also misunderstand them today. We need to learn about interpretation.

This is especially important because we are removed from the original events and situations of the Bible by several thousand years, by our culture and by our language. There will certainly be things in the Bible that are difficult for us to understand and things that we can easily misunderstand. These may be cultural and historic references as well as concepts and words.

I had a vivid illustration of this when I was visiting an American friend called David. He gave me his wedding album to look at. As I paged through it, I came across a photograph of David dancing with an elderly lady, with his arm around her waist. Being an African from the Busoga culture, I wondered what was going on. I asked him, "Who is this elderly lady you are dancing with?" To my utter consternation David answered, "My mother-in-law."

What a difference culture makes! In my culture, it is unthinkable even to lock eyes with my mother-in-law when conversing with her from a distance. Dancing with her would be unheard of, and even evil! The possibility of doing so cannot cross my mind. It is easier to think of walking to the moon! But there was David dancing with his mother-in-law.

Suppose someone wrote about that wedding, and said, "David danced with his mother-in-law for about five minutes. Then they rejoined their friends at the table." A Musoga would interpret this as saying that David was a pervert! But David was actually a godly guy, doing what was customary in his culture. What he was doing does not violate the word of God.

Can you see how easy it can be for us, who are far removed from the culture of Bible times, to misinterpret a book that was written in foreign languages thousands of years ago?

Different Meanings

Another contemporary example may help to drive this point home: An American missionary returned home after spending many years in Africa. Greeting some acquaintance there, he said, "I feel really gay today," meaning that he was feeling happy. The people listening to him were dumbfounded! "How could this man of God say such a thing? Is he gay – a homosexual? What a let-down!" The word "gay" had taken on a new and more prominent meaning during the many years the missionary had been away. There was a gap in language and time, and his words needed to be interpreted.

The same situation can arise in Africa. I remember passing a bar on the main road from Jinja to Malaba and Busia on the Kenya/Uganda border in the 1960s. It was called the Gay Life Bar. Forty years later that bar is still there, with its name still prominently displayed. Many foreign visitors from the USA and Europe travel along this road, and I often wonder what they think when they see Gay Life Bar in Jinja! They may conclude that homosexuality is quite acceptable in Uganda. Nothing could be further from the truth!

The meaning of the word "gay" has evolved. In the 1980s, the *World Book Dictionary* could still define it as "happy and full of fun; merry". By the 1990s the *Longman Dictionary of Contemporary English* prominently defined it as "homosexual". Whenever we come across a word, we need to check when and where it is being used. The context really matters. If we fall into the trap of assuming that it has its familiar and general meaning, we may misinterpret what is being said.

One final example of the pitfalls of assuming the familiar meaning of a phrase: I remember taking a mock biology practical examination in 1969. We were given a bone and told, "Draw the side-view of this bone." These were all familiar words – perhaps too familiar. Many students who were not good at drawing decided it meant draw the "view from the side" – any side! So they turned the bone this way and that way to find the easiest side to draw. They balanced it upright, turned it round and round, and viewed it from many and varied angles. But they were wrong, and they all failed the examination. Our biology teacher was not amused. In biology, there is a particular view of the bone called the "side-view". It is "a surface of the bone that is not its front, back, top, or bottom".

Interpretation Has Always Been Necessary

The Bible itself tells us that interpretation has always been necessary. Consider Ezra and the Levites who "read from the Book of the Law of God, making it clear and giving the meaning so that the people understood what was being read" (Neh 8:8). Note what Ezra and the Levites did: they made the law clear and explained its meaning. This is a concise description of what interpretation involves.

3

DEFINITION OF INTERPRETATION

It is important to define what we mean by "interpretation" because we need to know what we are talking about and be sure that we are talking about the same thing. Basically, interpretation asks the question, "What does this mean?" But such a simple definition needs further clarification. We can start by looking at what it does *not* mean.

Interpretation Is Not About What It Means to Me

The Basoga of Uganda have a saying, *Omutamivu awuliramu kirala* ("someone who is drunk hears only one word in a conversation"). A drunken man focuses only on the word that happens to catch his attention, regardless of what the speaker is actually trying to say. For example, suppose you were to read John 13:27 to someone who is drunk: "Then Jesus said to Judas, 'What you are about to do, do quickly.'" The person might only hear, "What you are about to do, do quickly", and rush off to get another drink. That would be his interpretation, although it is not at all what Jesus was talking about. But the only meaning that matters to the drunken man is what he thinks it means, regardless of the context!

This example shows the danger of thinking that the correct interpretation of a text is "what it means to me". Unfortunately, however, this is how many approach the Bible. Ralph Martin calls it the "impressionistic approach":

> Its main characteristic is a way of approaching ... Scripture in which the reader equates the message of the passage before him with the thoughts which fill his mind as he reads. The exercise is one of gaining impressions from the text, which has its function in exciting and engendering a series of "thoughts", triggered by the verses in question. This is a popular treatment of the Bible.[1]

This approach makes interpretation a wholly subjective exercise, based only on people's feelings and thoughts. As a result, there can be as many interpretations of a passage as there are interpreters. This, of course, would be wrong. The impressionistic approach is misleading, chaotic and confusing. Martin correctly objects to it as, "a treatment of Scripture which is at the mercy of human feelings; it fails to submit to some objective control in a recognition of the plain sense of the text, set in its historical context".[2]

Once when I was waiting outside the General Post Office in Kampala, Uganda, two men were standing talking near me. They were encouraging each other in the Lord. I overheard one of them say:

> Brother, I was recently in deep financial need and I was feeling very low. I just happened to open the Bible to Psalm 2:8. Do you know what it says? "Ask of me, and I will make the nations your heritage, and the ends of the earth your possession." You see, God promised here to give me the whole wide world. What is this little financial problem?"

Good sentiment – wrong text!

This man was misinterpreting and misapplying a text in which God promises that his anointed Davidic king will inherit and rule the whole world. My brother should have quoted other verses that speak of God's care for his children and his generous provision for our needs. For example:

> Now to him who is able to do immeasurably more than all we
> ask or imagine, according to his power that is at work within
> us. (Eph 3:20)

> Cast all your anxiety on him because he cares for you.
> (1 Pet 5:7)

That man is not alone in making this mistake. Many of us would interpret
Psalm 2:8 in the same way and use it to preach thrilling sermons.
However, we would be acting like the drunken man who misinterprets
Jesus' words and quickly goes off to get a drink. The fact that Jesus
was speaking to Judas might entirely escape his attention! What might
escape our attention here is that the Lord is directing his wonderful
decree in Psalm 2:8 to the Messiah and not to us.

Interpretation Is Not About What It Meant to the Original Audience

Interpretation is also not necessarily what the text meant to the original
audience. Now, this statement can be controversial because some
eminent scholars base much of their interpretation of Scripture on what
the original audience understood.[3] However, though the understanding
of the original audience is helpful, it does not necessarily give us the
correct interpretation. Let us look again at the examples we mentioned
earlier.

In John 21:22–23 the disciples were Jesus' original audience, but
they misunderstood what Jesus meant, even though he was speaking to
Peter face to face in their hearing. Jesus told Peter, "If I want him [John]
to remain alive until I return, what is that to you? You must follow me."
These words led to a rumour that John would never die. But this was a
misinterpretation of Jesus' words. The original audience was wrong and
it would be wrong to accept their interpretation.

In 1 Corinthians 5:9–10, the original audience of one of Paul's letters
misunderstood what he was telling them. He had instructed them not
to associate with "sexually immoral people". The Corinthians thought
that he was telling them not to associate with unbelievers, the people of
this world. So Paul corrects them and says that their interpretation was

wrong. So, you see again that the original audience can make wrong interpretations.

But even our everyday conversation makes this clear. We have all had the experience of correcting someone we have been speaking to, "No, no, no. You misunderstood me!" We all know that the original audience sometimes gets it wrong.

It should also be noted that the original recipients were not just passive listeners but also interpreters. If we base our interpretations solely on their interpretations of what was said, we are assuming that the author communicated perfectly with the audience. That is not always the case, as the examples above indicate.

As George Ladd insightfully remarks, "On a purely human level, a teacher can transcend his environment with original and novel insights; this is particularly important in the matter of divine revelation."[4]

Interpretation is not what the text means to me nor is it necessarily what the text meant to the original audience.

Interpretation Is About What the Author Meant

Interpretation is what the author meant. This is the meaning that the interpreter seeks.[5] So, when you read Scripture you should be asking, "What did the writer of this psalm mean? What did the writer of this letter mean? What did the writer of this book mean?" and so on. You are seeking the meaning that the author intended.

Let's give an example: A story is told of an old man who found a newspaper and read it. It contained a news item: "Tomorrow the king will be visiting our town … People are urged to turn out in large numbers to welcome him." The town that was mentioned happened to be the town where the old man lived. So he eagerly prepared to go and welcome his king. Alas, although he waited all day, the king never came.

To interpret what he was reading correctly, the old man should have gone beyond the dictionary meaning of "tomorrow" ("the day after today") and checked the date of the newspaper. That would have given him the context to enable him to identify the referent, that is, the person or day or thing to which the text was referring. If the newspaper was published on Monday, 30 July 2007, the "tomorrow" referred to in the item about the king was Tuesday, 31 July 2007, which was long in the past. The old man could have spared himself empty excitement and confusion by simply identifying the referent.

> **The goal of interpretation is to go beyond the lexical or dictionary meaning to the "referent" – the thing or person to whom the text refers.**

A biblical example of the same problem is found in Judges 1:20–21, which says,

> As Moses had promised, Hebron was given to Caleb, who drove from it the three sons of Anak. The Benjamites, however, did not drive out the Jebusites, who were living in Jerusalem; to this day the Jebusites live there with the Benjamites.

The dictionary meaning of "to this day" would be today, the time we are living in. But interpretation requires us to go beyond the dictionary meaning and find out what day the writer was referring to. Our knowledge of when the book of Judges was written tells us that the referent of "this day" lies in the distant past.

Another biblical example is in John 16:7. There Jesus says,

> But I tell you the truth: It is for your good that I am going away. Unless I go away, the Counsellor will not come to you; but if I go, I will send him to you (NIV).

The dictionary meaning of "counsellor" is "someone who comes alongside to give help and support." But you cannot stop here. You need to be able to identify the specific person whom the text is referring to as "the Counsellor". Some have been known to say that the Counsellor who Jesus says is coming is none other than their own teacher! This reminds us that it is important in interpretation to go beyond the dictionary meaning to the referent – the person or thing to which the text refers, as much as the context allows.

In the case of John 16:7, the context clearly specifies who this Counsellor is. Jesus has already mentioned him earlier in this *same conversation* on the *same subject*. In John 15:26 he told his disciples that the Counsellor whom he will send will testify about him, that this Counsellor is the "Spirit of truth", and that this Counsellor proceeds from the Father.

Earlier, Jesus also talked about this Counsellor as the Holy Spirit whom the Father will send for the disciples, and said that this Counsellor will teach the disciples all things (John 14:26). Still earlier, Jesus talked of the Counsellor as being given from the Father and referred to him as the "Spirit of truth" (John 14:16–17), the same title he used in John 15:26.

All of this evidence shows that the promised Counsellor in John 16:7 is the Holy Spirit. He is the referent. It is not enough simply to interpret "Counsellor" in John 16:7 as someone who comes alongside to help or support. We need to go beyond the dictionary meaning and recognize that Jesus is referring to none other than the Holy Spirit.

I have a personal example of what can happen if we do not correctly identify the referent. There was a dispute about a health unit in a remote village in my diocese. The local government chief thought that he had authority over it, but it was actually under the authority of the parish priest and the parish council of the church. Ultimate authority for the clinic rested with the diocesan office.

To resolve this issue, the diocese wrote to the priest as follows: "The parish has authority over the health unit". This letter was copied to the government chief in the area. With his copy of the letter in hand, the chief proceeded to fire the nurse in charge of the health unit, saying that the diocesan letter confirmed that his "parish" was in charge!

When I visited the local church as the bishop, the priest brought this matter up, pleading that the diocese should clarify who actually was in charge – the church as the "parish" or the chief's area, which was also referred to as a "parish" by the government. The dictionary meaning of "parish" provided no help in solving this dispute. It actually caused confusion and almost led to a riot and violence.

In interpretation, you ought to go beyond the dictionary meaning and use the context to identify the referent, the person or thing the author was referring to.

Interpretation asks the question, "What does it mean?" Identifying the referent helps the interpreter find out what the author specifically intended.

Now, all Scripture is inspired by God. So, when it comes to Scripture there are two authors: a human author and the divine author. These two never contradict each other, although sometimes the divine author intends a referent that is grander and deeper than the human author realized. This happens where we have prophecies, types or prefigurements of what is to come or what will be re-enacted later on a grander scale. For example, when the ancient writers of the Old Testament referred to a sacrificial lamb, they were thinking only of an animal. But then Jesus came as "the Lamb of God, who takes away the sin of the world" (John 1:29). So, at a deeper level, the sacrificial lamb in the Old Testament prefigured Christ himself as the ultimate referent.

It is important to note that where there is a deeper referent or meaning, Scripture itself must point it out. The fundamental principle is that Scripture interprets Scripture. This principle eliminates fantastic and sometimes bizarre interpretations, such as the idea that the five stones David picked up to fight Goliath (1 Sam 17:40) refer to the five books of Moses or that the red piece of cloth Rahab hung in her window (Josh 2:18) refers to the blood of Christ. Where is the scriptural basis for these interpretations? They are based solely on individual imagination and coincidence.

On the other hand, Scripture clearly points out the deeper meaning or referent when Caiaphas, the high priest, said, "You do not realize that it is better for you that one man die for the people than that the whole nation perish" (John 11:50). Caiaphas, the human author, as it were, was referring to the nation of Israel, just like the divine author. But the divine author intended his words to be a prophecy with a far grander referent than Caiaphas knew. Scripture itself spells this out:

> He [Caiaphas] did not say this on his own, but as high priest that year he prophesied that Jesus would die for the Jewish nation, and not only for that nation but also for the scattered children of God, to bring them together and make them one. (John 11:51–52)

Scripture interprets Scripture. Scripture itself is the sure guide to interpretation and its sure foundation – not personality, imagination and coincidences!

4

METHODS OF INTERPRETATION

Having learned what interpretation is about, it is now time to discuss some approaches to interpretation. How do we set about determining what the author actually meant? What methods can we use?

Methods are like glasses. If we are wearing coloured glasses, everything we see will be tinted by the colour of our glasses. If they are clear, we will see the object as it really is. In the same way, the method of interpretation we choose will affect how clearly we can see the text. We thus need to be careful of the method we use in interpretation.

There are three main methods we will discuss: the allegorical method, the historical-critical method and the historical-grammatical method. You should note that the interpreter or preacher may not state what method is being used. You need to be able to discern this for yourself.

The Allegorical Method

The allegorical method of interpretation goes beyond the text and comes up with fantastic meanings. It is completely subjective – the interpretation depends on the individual and their imagination. It is also arbitrary – the person does not follow any rules of interpretation and cannot give you clear details from the text to support their interpretation. Instead, there is a lot of spiritualizing and taking things out of context. Ideas and interpretations are triggered by coincidences and remote associations, without any regard for the context.

Let me give you an example of this method. Once when I was conducting a workshop on interpretation I asked one of the participants, whom we can call George, to conduct an evening devotion. For his text, George chose Acts 12:1–11, which tells the story of how an angel of the Lord rescued Peter from prison. In verse 8 the angel says to Peter, "Put on your clothes and sandals ... Wrap your cloak around you and follow me."

Then George said this: "When the angel told Peter to put on his sandals, he was exhorting him to always be prepared with the gospel of peace, for Ephesians 6:15 says that our feet are to be 'shod with the preparation of the gospel of peace'" (KJV).

Wow! I could see that the class was impressed by this interpretation. But it was all allegorical and was taking things completely out of context. The angel was telling Peter that he needed to get dressed so that he could walk out of prison and go back to his friends. George, however, spiritualized the matter. His ideas were triggered by nothing more than the coincidence that the word "feet" appeared in both verses.

Now, suppose there was a story like this: "Joshua performed very well at college and was head of his class at graduation. The head of state, who was guest of honour at the graduation, gave Joshua an award for his excellent performance." Would you conclude that the head of state was also the cleverest person in the state simply because the word "head" was also applied to him? No, not at all! The word must be taken in its context, one being academic achievement and the other being a level of government authority.

Similarly, in the familiar story of David and Goliath we are told that David "chose five smooth stones from the stream" (1 Sam 17:40). In the last chapter I mentioned that some interpreters say that the "five" stones represent the five books of Moses. This is an allegorical interpretation. It takes the coincidence that the number "five" applies to both and spiritualizes it.

This transference of meanings from one context to another simply because of coincidences is absurd. But it is typical of what happens when people rely on allegorical methods of interpretation.

Let me give you another example: I heard someone teaching on leadership. He quoted Revelation 1:10–12, where it says, "On the Lord's Day I was in the Spirit, and I heard behind me a loud voice like a trumpet … I turned around to see the voice that was speaking to me." Then he asked the audience, "Can you see a voice?" The audience replied, "No." Then he said, "So when the Bible says that the Apostle John turned to see the voice, it is not talking about him physically turning his head! It is talking about the flexibility of his leadership style!"

Wow! First, this teacher is misinterpreting a figure of speech, that is, a common way of speaking. When someone says, "I can see what you're thinking", she is using a figure of speech. Thoughts cannot be seen; the saying means, "I understand you". In the same way, when John turned "to see the voice", he was turning his head to see who the voice came from, or in other words, who was speaking.

Second, the teacher associates John's turning his head with a flexible leadership style. While there is a remote connection between turning one's head and changing one's mind, when we read the verse in context it is clear that John is simply turning around to see the person speaking. He is not changing his mind or being flexible in his thinking. The teacher's interpretation is allegorical; it spiritualizes things and takes them out of context.

The allegorical method of interpretation has a long history. It was popular among ancient rabbis and some church fathers.[6] For example Saint Augustine (AD 354–430) used this method to interpret the parable of the Good Samaritan:

> A certain man went down from Jerusalem to Jericho; Adam himself is meant; Jerusalem is the heavenly city of peace, from whose blessedness Adam fell; Jericho means the moon, and signifies our mortality, because it is born, waxes, wanes, and dies. Thieves are the devil and his angels. Who stripped him, namely, of his immortality; and beat him, by persuading him to sin, and left him half-dead, because in so far as man can understand and know God, he lives, but in so far as he is wasted and oppressed by sin, he is dead; he is therefore called half-dead. The priest and Levite who saw him and passed by signify the priesthood and ministry of the Old Testament.[7]

This interpretation is subjective. It derives purely from Augustine's own ingenuity and imagination. Sadly, it also results in Jesus' ethical teaching on love for our neighbour being all but buried.

But before we point fingers at St. Augustine, we need to remember that even today many of us interpret the parables using the allegorical method. When we do this, we are forgetting that each parable has a central theme that is clear from the context in which it is told. If we do not focus on this theme when we interpret the parable, we can end up assigning all kinds of fantastic meanings to the details.

> **Every parable has a central theme that is apparent from the context and should be interpreted in terms of this theme.**

I will end this section with one final example of a sermon based on allegorical interpretation. The pastor, whom I will call Joel, had been in ministry for over thirty-five years. For his text he chose Ezra 8:21–22, which records Ezra's praying before he set out on his journey to Jerusalem:

> Then I proclaimed a fast there, at the river Aha'va, that we might humble ourselves before our God, to seek from him a straight way for ourselves, our children, and all our goods. For I was ashamed to ask the king for a band of soldiers and horsemen to protect us against the enemy on our way; since we had told the king, "The hand of our God is for good upon all that seek him, and the power of his wrath is against all that forsake him."

Joel seized upon the word "way" in the text and ran with it. He preached a thrilling sermon, saying that Ezra prayed for a straight way, the way of salvation. Joel preached that Ezra was aware of the many enemies and dangers on this straight way, the way of salvation, and that we should always remember that Jesus is "the way and the truth and the life" (John 14:6) and take refuge in him.

The people praised Joel for such a nice sermon. Well, nice sermon – wrong text. It was all allegorizing. Joel transferred meanings from one context to another on account of coincidences in the words used. Ezra was clearly praying for a safe journey back to Jerusalem. But seeing the word *way* took Joel all the way to John 14:6!

Unfortunately, allegorical interpretation is widespread today. Some of it is off the wall and absurd; some of it is more sophisticated. But all of it is subjective.

The allegorical method takes things out of context and spiritualizes them. It relies on ideas triggered by coincidences and remote associations.

The Historical-Critical Method

The second approach we will consider is the historical-critical method, which arose out of the Enlightenment in Germany in the eighteenth century and is prevalent in scholarship today.

The historical-critical method asks two questions: a) What does the witness say? (In other words, what does the text in the Bible say?); b) What is the value of this witness? (In other words, how do we evaluate what it says?) This second question explains why this method is called a "critical" method. What the Bible says is not taken at face value. Instead, it is treated like a witness in a court of law. After the witness has given his or her evidence, a judge evaluates what has been said. If the witness is thought to be biased or lack integrity, what he or she says will not be taken at face value.

The historical-critical method can be applied to any of the many books written over the course of history. But there is a problem when it is applied to the Bible because this method is naturalistic and anti-supernatural. Scholars who use it treat the Bible as simply a product of its times and regard the biblical authors as simply reflecting the prejudices and understandings of their times. These scholars argue that "the Bible ought to be interpreted like any other book".[8] The interpreter is the judge of the text.

Let's look at some examples where the historical-critical method is used. We can begin with what *The Interpreter's Bible* has to say about the following verse from Matthew's gospel:

> After Jesus was born in Bethlehem in Judea, during the time of King Herod, Magi from the east came to Jerusalem and asked, "Where is the one who has been born king of the Jews? We saw his star when it rose and have come to worship him" (Matt 2:1–2).

The Interpreter's Bible comments on and interprets these verses as follows:

> The adoration of the magi, like the other narratives in this chapter, has no parallel in other first-century Christian writing. There is thus no way to ascertain whether it has been embellished, or indeed, whether it "happened" at all as a matter of literal fact. The value and importance of the narrative do not depend on its accuracy; the story is rather to be thought of as a work of art, which the evangelist presents to the Christ child as his offering. Christians who hear it read during Christmas or Epiphany season instinctively recognise its value, regardless of the question of fact. It expresses the truth that men have been brought from afar and by many ways to worship Christ.[9]

This is a very typical example of the historical-critical method. *The Interpreter's Bible* does not take what Matthew says at face value. It judges his words and declares that this event never actually happened. Matthew just created a beautiful story. The commentary even tells us what Matthew's motive was: he wanted to create "a work of art" that he could offer to the Christ child.

Not content just to tell us what Matthew was "really" thinking, the commentary also tells us what you and I and all other Christians think: none of us care whether the story is true, or whether it actually happened! The real value of the story (and here comes the interpretation) is that "it expresses the truth that men have been brought from afar and by many ways to worship Christ."

Let's look at another example of the historical-critical method from *The Interpreter's Bible*. In 1 Timothy 2:11–12, the Bible says, "A woman should learn in quietness and full submission. I do not permit a woman to teach or to have authority over a man; she must be silent." Now, this is what *The Interpreter's Bible* says about these verses:

> The present passage would represent a later and more conservative position with regard to women in church than that of Paul ... In part this may have been caused by extravagances resulting from the primitive Christian "emancipation" of women, in part by a natural masculine reluctance to yield historic prerogatives to women.[10]

Here, the interpreter judges that Paul did not write these verses. He argues that they were written after Paul's time by Christians who merely reflect the prejudices of their conservative camp. Consequently, the interpreter says, this passage does not speak with any authority.

In the historical-critical method, the interpreter is a judge of the text.

We see the same dismissal of biblical texts in the raging debate about homosexuality and sin. A young girl once asked me, "Don't those who say that homosexuality is not sin read the Bible? The Bible clearly condemns homosexuality in Sodom and Gomorrah." She pointed to Genesis 19:5–8:

> They called to Lot, "Where are the men who came to you tonight? Bring them out to us so that we can have sex with them." Lot went outside to meet them and shut the door behind him and said, "No, my friends. Don't do this wicked thing. Look, I have two daughters who have never slept with a man. Let me bring them out to you, and you can do whatever you like with them."

She then pointed to another scripture, "Look at what Romans 1:26–27 says:"

> Because of this, God gave them over to shameful lusts. Even their women exchanged natural relations for unnatural ones. In the same way the men also abandoned natural relations with women and were inflamed with lust for one another. Men committed shameful acts with other men, and received in themselves the due penalty for their error.

She asked me again, "Don't they read the Bible?" I answered her, "The problem is with the method they use. It's all in the method!"

Soon after this, I had a conversation with a churchman, well-schooled in the Scriptures. He told me, "Nowhere in the Bible is homosexuality condemned as sin." I was totally taken aback! I quickly pointed out the story of Sodom and Gomorrah in Genesis 19 and what Paul says in Romans 1. We debated the interpretation of these passages for over four hours, but I could not convince him. Then it hit me, and I remembered what I had said to the young girl: "The problem is with the method. It's all in the method!"

The Historical-Grammatical Method

The final method we will consider is the historical-grammatical method. This method seeks the plain and normal meaning of a passage in its context, while taking into account the rules of grammar and figures of speech. This is the method that evangelicals generally subscribe to.

It must be pointed out that the historical-grammatical method is similar to the historical-critical method in that both consider the context, the rules of grammar, figures of speech and historical background. The important difference is that the historical-critical method is naturalistic and anti-supernatural, and sits in judgment of the text. It does not take the text at face value but judges it and decides whether to accept what the text says or not. On the other hand, the historical-grammatical method believes in the supernatural and that Scripture is inspired by God. It takes Scripture at face value – it accepts what the text says and does not explain it away.

I take the historical-grammatical approach to interpretation, and this is the method we will dwell on in this book.

5

IMPORTANCE OF OBSERVATION

I was once part of an evangelistic mission in Kampala, Uganda, in which we were sent out in twos to share the gospel. My partner, who was called James, came from western Uganda and spoke Kinyankole. However, the community in central Uganda that we were sent to spoke Luganda, a language James did not know well. But there are similarities between Kinyankole and Luganda, and so James tried to share the gospel using a mixture of broken Luganda and Kinyankole.

Unfortunately some words in Kinyankole have entirely different meanings in Luganda. So when James told a small group, *Bwoyagala okutunga Yesu* his audience burst into laughter. What James was saying in Kinyankole was "if you want to have Jesus ..." but in Luganda the words meant "If you want to sew Jesus up ...". No wonder his audience was amused! They thought that James was crazy.

If only they had done a little observation. Just by looking at James they should have been able to tell that he came from western Uganda. His accent and his broken Luganda were also telling signs that he was a Munyankole who knew little Luganda and was struggling to communicate a message in it.

What the audience should have done was ask a few observation questions like: "*Who* is this man? *Where* does he come from? I can tell he is from western Uganda and he knows little Luganda. Is he using a Kinyankole word? I wonder *what* 'okutunga' means in Kinyankole?"

By asking these observation questions – "who, what, where" – they would have discovered that in Kinyankole the word "okutunga" means "to have or to find". James was talking about finding salvation in Jesus, not about sewing Jesus up!

This story illustrates that observation is the foundation of interpretation, whether we are interpreting a conversation or a written text. By "observation" I mean "paying attention" to the text, that is, being alert and very observant of the text.

> **Observation is the foundation of interpretation in the sense that good interpretation proceeds from good observation.**

Do you remember the man we referred to earlier who read in an old newspaper that the king was coming to his town? The man made all the preparations and went out the following day to welcome his king. Alas, the king never came! If only the man had done a little observation! If he had, he would not have come up with his totally false interpretation of what the newspaper said. If only he had asked, "*What* is the date of this newspaper?" or "*When* was this article written?" He would have known that the king had already come to the town many years ago. The event was already past!

We have already seen that the goal of interpretation goes beyond the dictionary meaning of a word to who or what is the referent, the person or thing specifically referred to. Asking the observation question, "What is the date of this newspaper?" would have helped the man know that that "tomorrow" was no longer "the day after today". It was a specific day, and it was already past.

Good Observation Leads to Good Interpretation

You need to be alert and observant as you read and interpret a text, or any conversation for that matter. You will find it helpful to ask the following observation questions:

Who?   What?   When?
Where?   Why?   How?

Let us look at some practical examples of how to do this. In this example, you should also note that we define and isolate the interpretive issue, that is, the particular problem we want to solve. This is important in any interpretive debate, so that you do not go all over the place and confuse matters.

Luke 17:21 can be translated as "the kingdom of God is within you" or "the kingdom of God is among you". Thus the interpretive issue is which word Jesus meant, "among" or "within"? To solve the problem, we need to ask and answer some observation questions.

- *Who* was speaking? Jesus was speaking.
- *Why* was he speaking? He was answering a question.
- *What* question? The question was when the kingdom of God would come.
- *Who* asked this question? The Pharisees.
- *What* were the Pharisees? They were a religious group.
- *How* did they view Jesus? They viewed him with hostility. They were not his followers or believers.
- *What* was Jesus? He was the Messiah, the Davidic king who was to come and usher in the kingdom of God. He is the king of the kingdom of God.

Once we have made these observations (and any others you think necessary), we can move on to interpret Jesus' words and answer the question of what Jesus really meant. Was it that "the kingdom of God is *within* you" or that "the kingdom of God is *among* you"? Would Jesus say that the kingdom of God was "within" the Pharisees? If so, he was talking about a spiritual kingdom, perhaps the reign of God in people's hearts. But these Pharisees were hostile to Jesus. They were opposing him and his message of the kingdom. Would Jesus say that God was reigning in their hearts? That seems unlikely.

Did Jesus mean that the kingdom of God was "among" the Pharisees? Well, Jesus was the Messiah, the king of the kingdom of God and he was right there among them. So this interpretation seems more likely.

This example shows how careful observation helps interpretation.

Observation Includes Grammar

We need to pay attention to things like figures of speech, as we did in the previous chapter in relation to Revelation, where a teacher made much of the Apostle John turning his head "to see the voice" that spoke with him. And we also need to look at the grammar, including things like the tense of verbs and the conjunctions that link sentences and ideas.

Let's look again at our earlier example of the disciples' misunderstanding of Jesus' words about John (John 21:21–23). Peter asked Jesus about John, saying, "Lord, what about him?" Jesus answered, "If I want him to remain alive until I return, what is that to you?" When the disciples interpreted this exchange, they ignored the tiny conjunction "If". So they assumed that John would not die before Jesus' return. But what Jesus had actually said was "*If* I want him to remain alive until I return, what is that to you?" There would have been no misinterpretation if the disciples had taken the trouble to observe the conjunction.

We should define and isolate the interpretive issues so that we do not get distracted and confused.

Another of our earlier examples of misunderstanding involved people who did not pay enough attention to matters of grammar when they interpreted the Scriptures. Jesus corrected the Sadducees' faulty theology about the resurrection by asking them, "Have you not read what God said to you, 'I am the God of Abraham, the God of Isaac, and the God of Jacob'? He is not the God of the dead but of the living" (Matt 22:29–31). The Sadducees denied that there was life after death, but they had failed to observe that God used the present tense when he said, "I *am* the God of Abraham". He did not use the past tense: "I *was* the God of Abraham". Abraham, Isaac and Jacob must still be alive, for God "is not the God of the dead, but of the living."

Practise Observation

Observation is a critical step in interpretation. It should be done carefully, not casually or hurriedly. You should read, read and reread the passage. Be alert and pay attention to the terms used, to which terms are connected to each other and to the nature of the connection, to figures of speech, matters of grammar, matters of background and context, the type of literature involved (narrative, wisdom, epistle, apocalyptic), the people and personalities involved, the atmosphere, and so on.

I recommend that you make your observations first and then move on to interpretation. However, you can note down interpretation questions like, "What is the meaning or significance of this term?" if they come to mind at the observation stage. They can be picked up again at the interpretation stage.

Let us look at two more examples. If you want to, you could try and do your own observations and interpretations of them first, before reading what I have written here.

John 5:24

> Very truly, I tell you, whoever hears my words and believes him who sent me has eternal life and will not be judged, but has crossed over from death to life.

- *What* are some of the words we observe? "Very truly" (some translations say "Truly, truly"), "eternal life", "judged" and "death".
- *How* are these ideas connected? Jesus uses the word "but" when he says the believer will not be judged "but has crossed over from death to life."
- *Who* is speaking? Jesus is speaking.
- *To whom* is Jesus speaking? He is speaking to the Jews.
- *What* is the atmosphere like? The Jews are hostile to Jesus. They want to kill him and refuse to listen to him because he called God his father (verse 18).

- *What* can we observe about the grammar? Jesus uses the present tense: "whoever believes ... *has* eternal life". He also says that the believer "has crossed over from death to life", using the perfect tense.

These are just some of the possible observations on John 5:24. You can probably make many more.

Now, how do these observations help us when we set out to interpret the passage?

First, we can tell that what Jesus has to say here is not ordinary or routine stuff that his hearers would already know. That is why he has to start by getting their attention with "very truly" (or "truly, truly"). These words indicate that he wants them to listen carefully to what he has to say.

Second, we can say that Jesus told them something extraordinary. He told them about eternal life.

Third, he used the present tense, which conveys the amazing news that eternal life is not something you get in the future; it is something you have now, when you believe!

Fourth, he explains something about what eternal life involves. He does this by using the word "but" to establish a contrast between those who are judged and those who believe in him. The former are judged, but the latter have "crossed over from death to life". So the judgment is not simply a matter of determining whether people are right or wrong about something. It involves the difference between being alive and being dead.

As we carry on interpreting this passage, we will see that what Jesus is talking about is eternal salvation. There is now no condemnation for the believer. Sins are forgiven in Christ. The believer is righteous in Christ and will live forever with God in heaven.

Matthew 28:18–20

> Then Jesus came to them and said, "All authority in heaven and on earth has been given to me. Therefore go and make disciples of all nations, baptizing them in the name of the Father and of the Son and of the Holy Spirit, and teaching them to obey everything I have commanded you. And surely I am with you always, to the very end of the age."

- *Who* is speaking? Jesus is speaking.
- *To whom* is he speaking? He is speaking to the eleven disciples, who were Jews like Jesus.
- *Where* did this take place? In Galilee, in Israel.
- *When* did it take place? In ancient Israel, about two thousand years ago.
- *What* was the atmosphere like? It must have been sombre, for Jesus was about to leave the disciples and these were his final words to them.
- *How* did Jesus start his instruction to his disciples? He started by pointing out his authority.
- *What* did he say about his authority? It is "all" authority "in heaven and on earth"; this authority "has been given" to him.
- *What* are some other important terms to observe? "Make disciples" is the main action in the instruction, qualified by "baptizing them" and "teaching them to obey everything I have commanded".
- *What* can we notice about the grammar? The sentences are joined by the conjunction "therefore".
- *What* is the significance of "therefore"? This is a question we will answer when we interpret the passage.
- *What* does Jesus promise? Jesus promises his presence "always, to the very end of the age".
- *What* is the significance of Jesus' promise? This question, too, involves interpretation.

We can now use these observations to do a little interpretation of Matthew 28:18–20. We will keep it simple for the sake of illustration.

First, Jesus starts by pointing out his authority. This authority is awesome and unfathomable – it is "all" authority in heaven and on earth. This is absolute authority, above all others. Jesus then says, "therefore", and gives the commission. The word "therefore" points back to his authority; Jesus is invoking his absolute and awesome authority in giving this commission. This is something that should hold the disciples' full attention – even more so because the atmosphere was sombre because these were Jesus' last words.

Second, Jesus instructs his disciples to "make disciples". Jesus is a Jew, and he is talking to his disciples, who were also Jews, in an ancient Jewish context. So to understand what he means we need to learn a little more about the ancient Jewish concept of discipleship. It involved a lot more than simply attending Bible studies and doing some ministry together. For the Jews, being a disciple meant being devoted to one's teacher and striving to be like him.

Third, this command to make disciples extends to "all nations". So it will involve going to the nations as well as baptizing and teaching them.

Fourth, with the commission Jesus gives a promise. He prefaces this promise with the word "surely", which underlines what he is saying and makes it clear that it is of special significance. He says, "Surely, "I am with you always, to the very end of the age." This promise has special significance, because if the all-powerful Jesus is with them, they will succeed in carrying out his commission. This promise should also be a comfort to the disciples because this awesome task is not left to them alone; Jesus' presence, his enabling provision, is with them. And he is not just with them now and then but always. He is not with them for a temporary period but "to the very end of the age".

Fifth, the fact that Jesus says he will be with them "to the very end of the age" means that this commission is not only for the eleven disciples, who will sooner or later all die; it is for all disciples until the end of time.

To summarize, our observation of this passage shows that in giving his commission, Jesus invokes his awesome and almighty authority and promises that his almighty and enabling presence will always be with his disciples to the end of the age. These were Jesus' last words to his disciples. This commission to make disciples of all nations has rightly been called the "Great Commission".

Observation is a critical step in interpretation and it should be done carefully, not casually or hurriedly.

6

IMPORTANCE OF CONTEXT

I was once serving Holy Communion, using the method of dipping a little piece of bread in the wine and giving it to the person taking communion. When I came to one particular person, the priest who was assisting me said, "Bishop, that one likes to *drink*." Now, do you think the priest was reporting a Christian who liked alcohol? No! He was simply telling me that some people in that church preferred to take the bread first and then drink from the cup. If I had not paid attention to the context, I could have misunderstood the word "drink" and misjudged the person.

This story illustrates the importance of context. Context determines the meaning of a passage or term. Yes. Context is that important. It is crucial to meaning. Yet it is amazing how often context is overlooked, not just by the untrained but even by teachers and preachers of the word, people who should know better.

Without context, it can be impossible to know exactly what even a simple sentence means. For example, consider this sentence: "He is running." Does it mean that he is moving at a pace faster than walking? Does it mean that he is in a hurry? Or does it mean that he is a candidate in an election? The only way to know what is meant is to know the context of that sentence. If the context is political, then the meaning would be, "He is a candidate in a political race".

Context and Simple Passages

The examples above show how much we rely on context in ordinary conversations. We also need it when interpreting the Bible. Let's start by looking at two very straightforward examples to drive the point home that context determines the meaning of a passage or term. Consider the term "asleep" in the following verses:

> While the women were on their way, some of the guards went into the city and reported to the chief priests everything that had happened. When the chief priests had met with the elders and devised a plan, they gave the soldiers a large sum of money, telling them, "You are to say, 'His disciples came during the night and stole him away while we were asleep.' If this report gets to the governor, we will satisfy him and keep you out of trouble." (Matt 28:11–14)

> Brothers, we do not want you to be ignorant about those who fall asleep, or to grieve like the rest of men, who have no hope. We believe that Jesus died and rose again and so we believe that God will bring with Jesus those who have fallen asleep in him. (1 Thess 4:13–14 NIV)

In Matthew, the context involves soldiers who are supposed to have been on guard at night. They are told to use the excuse that they were sleeping and did not notice what the disciples were up to. Here "asleep" clearly refers to physical sleep. In 1 Thessalonians, Paul is talking about our hope of resurrection and points to Jesus as his example. Given this context, "asleep" clearly means "dead". That is why the TNIV feels free to translate the opening words as "Brothers and sisters, we do not want you to be uninformed about those who sleep in death."

But suppose you had no context. Suppose you only had the sentence "He is asleep". It would not be easy to tell whether "asleep" means "not awake or sleeping; not aware; oblivious; unmindful or heedless" (as in "He is asleep to danger"); "dull or inactive" (as in "His mind is asleep"); and "dead", since the dictionary lists all of these as possible meanings.

   We can learn a lot from this simple example. A word can mean one thing here and another thing there. You should not assume that a word has only one meaning and carries this meaning every time it is used. If you do, you will be committing what is technically called the "prescriptive fallacy".

   It is very easy to fall into this fallacy – particularly when a word changes its meaning within the space of a few verses. Consider the two uses of the word "Greek" in Romans 1:14–16 (RSV):

> I am under obligation both to Greeks and to barbarians, both to the wise and to the foolish: so I am eager to preach the gospel to you also who are in Rome. (v. 14)

> For I am not ashamed of the gospel: it is the power of God for salvation to everyone who has faith, to the Jew first and also to the Greek. (v. 16)

In Paul's day many people thought of the world as divided into two classes: the wise and the foolish. Or, to put it another way, there were the Greeks (a people who were supposedly educated and civilized) and the barbarians (all other groups who were regarded as uncivilized and ignorant). So in verse 14 the word "Greeks" refers to the Greeks as a wise people.

   As a Jew, Paul would also have seen the world as divided into two religious categories: Jews and non-Jews. So "the Greek" in verse 16 means "everyone who isn't Jewish". That is why the TNIV translates this word as "the Gentile".

   The word "Greek" has two different meanings in the space of three verses! Without understanding the context of Paul's world, we would not have recognized this change. Context should be our sweet song in the interpretation of a passage or term.

Context determines the meaning of a passage or term.

Context and Complicated Passages

Sometimes our mistake is not that we ignore the context, but that we don't look at the context hard enough. The consequences can be serious, both for our interpretation and for our theology. Take, for example, the use of the word "justify".

In Romans and Galatians, Paul speaks about justification like this:

> For all have sinned and fall short of the glory of God, and all are justified freely by his grace through the redemption that came by Christ Jesus. (Rom 3:23–24)

> Know that a person is not justified by observing the law, but by faith in Jesus Christ. So we, too, have put our faith in Christ Jesus that we may be justified by faith in Christ and not by observing the law, because by observing the law no one will be justified. (Gal 2:16)

By contrast, James says:

> You see that people are justified by what they do and not by faith alone. (Jas 2:24)

If we assume that "justified" means exactly the same thing in all the passages quoted above, we have a problem – a big problem. Paul says that we cannot be justified by what we do, and James says that we are justified by what we do. Is Scripture contradicting Scripture? That cannot be! I will say it again: Scripture does not contradict Scripture. Remember that a presupposition of the historical-grammatical method of interpretation is that Scripture is inspired by God. If Scripture contradicts Scripture, God is contradicting himself, and that cannot be.

Martin Luther of the Protestant Reformation recognized the problem, and he solved it by dismissing the letter of James as "an epistle of straw" that did not belong in the Bible! Some other readers have decided that "justify" means the same thing in all of these passages, and they teach that we achieve salvation by a combination of "faith plus works". The result is an interpretive and theological tragedy!

But what does the word "justify" mean in all these passages? Remember what we said before: Context should be your sweet song as you interpret Scripture! Let us look at the context, and look hard.

In Romans and Galatians, Paul was answering the question, "How are we saved?" His answer was "only by faith in Jesus". James was answering a different question. The question he was dealing with was "What kind of faith saves?" His answer was "living faith, faith that works, faith that is evident in how you live".

Both Paul and James use the example of Abraham to shore up what they say about justification.

Paul says:

> What then shall we say that Abraham, the forefather of us Jews, discovered in this matter? If, in fact, Abraham was *justified* by works, he had something to boast about – but not before God. What does Scripture say? "Abraham believed God, and it was credited to him as righteousness."
>
> Now to anyone who works, their wages are not credited to them as a gift, but as an obligation. However, to anyone who does not work but trusts God who justifies the ungodly, their faith is credited as righteousness. (Rom 4:1–5)

James says,

> Was not Abraham our father justified by works, when he offered his son Isaac upon the altar? You see that faith was active along with his works, and faith was completed by works, and the scripture was fulfilled which says, "Abraham believed God, and it was reckoned to him as righteousness"; ... You see that a man is justified by works and not by faith alone. ... For as the body apart from the spirit is dead, so faith apart from works is dead. (Jas 2:21–26 RSV)

Paul argues that Abraham was "justified" when righteousness was credited to him as a gift because he believed God. He was not justified by faith plus works but by faith alone. Paul belaboured this same point in Galatians 2:16, quoted above. In this context, what does the term "justified" mean? It means "declared righteous". Paul is saying that Abraham was declared righteous when he believed what God said.

James' focus is on what it means to have faith. It is easy to say that you have faith, but if you have nothing to show for it, your faith is dead. On the other hand, you can have a faith that is alive. The proof that your faith is alive is that it is evident in what you do. So James asks, "Was not Abraham our father justified by works?" And he points to Abraham's faith: "and Scripture was fulfilled which says, 'Abraham believed God, and it was reckoned to him as righteousness'". The focus in James is on what kind of faith saves – faith that works.

In the context of James, what does the word "justified" mean? Does it mean "declared righteous"? Or does it mean "proved to be right"? Both meanings can be found in the dictionary. But here "proved to be right" fits the context better. Abraham proved that he believed in God by what he did. His belief in God showed. He was even willing to sacrifice his son, through whom God had promised him many descendants.

Regardless of whether the passage or word we are trying to understand is simple or complicated, we need to look at the context. In every case, context determines the meaning. This is true in all communication, even ordinary conversation.

Failure to scrutinize the context carefully can result in mistakes that have serious consequences for our interpretation and our theology.

Context Determines the Referent

Earlier I pointed out that the goal of interpretation is to go beyond the dictionary meaning of a word or expression to identify the "referent" – the thing or person specifically referred to. Here are two examples to refresh your memory of what that means.

In the movie *The Goonies* robbers chase a group of boys who have found a map showing where treasure has been hidden. The robbers want that map! Finally they corner one of the young boys and threaten him terribly. "Tell us *everything*!" they command. Trembling, the terrified boy says, "When I was little, I threw the cat down the stairs and blamed it on my baby sister."

The robbers were not amused. They wanted to know "everything", but they didn't mean every secret the boy could think of. In their context, "everything" meant *only* the details that would lead to where the map was hidden.

The dictionary meaning of "everything" is "all things" – whatever comes to mind. But the dictionary meaning made no sense in the context of the movie. The robbers wondered, "Throwing the cat down the stairs and blaming it on your baby sister – what has that got to do with anything?" When they said "everything", they meant "where the map is hidden". This was the referent, the meaning that goes beyond the dictionary meaning.

The second example comes from my own experience when I visited my friend Aggrey shortly after he had been admitted to hospital. I found him all alone in the room, sitting on a bed with no bedding. There was no one around to look after him. In Uganda, anyone who is admitted to a public hospital must have at least one family member or friend around to care for their needs.

I asked Aggrey, "Does *anyone* know that you are here?" He answered, "Oh yes. The doctor who admitted me and the ward staff know I'm here." I was amused. I was not asking whether he had sneaked into the hospital room. What I wanted to know was whether his family and friends knew he was there and would be coming to care for him. But Aggrey misunderstood what I meant by "anyone" because he did not consider the context and did not get the referents.

The goal of interpretation is to go beyond the dictionary meaning to the referent, the thing or person referred to. It is the context that determines the referent.

Let's consider a biblical example. In the Gospel of John, Jesus says:

> Very truly I tell you, my Father will give you whatever you ask
> in my name. (16:23)

Whatever we ask? Does that mean we can ask for anything we want? That is amazing! But does it really mean absolutely anything? What if I want to be a successful thief? Does this promise mean that he will give me the ability to do that?

To be able to answer the question, we have to start by making some observations. First of all, "Who is speaking?" Jesus is speaking. That straightaway puts us in the context of righteousness. "Whatever we ask" does not include things like "being a thief". The referent of "whatever" must be things that are righteous.

Next, we need to look at the context, and ask, "Has Jesus talked about this before or elsewhere in this conversation?" Looking at the whole conversation can give us more insight into what he means. I can illustrate this with a personal example. Just as I came up to two friends, the woman was saying, "My first duty is to my baby; no compromises!" I chipped in, "How about your husband?" She looked at me and said, "We were talking about my baby and my work." I said, "My apologies. I needed to hear the full conversation to get the context."

You need to hear the full conversation to get the full context.

Returning to the biblical example in John, we can ask, "Does Jesus talk about this before or elsewhere in this conversation?" Yes, he does. In the previous chapter Jesus says:

> You did not choose me, but I chose you and appointed you
> so that you might go and bear fruit – fruit that will last – and
> so that whatever you ask in my name the Father will give you.
> (John 15:16)

A few verses earlier, Jesus said something similar:

> If you remain in me and my words remain in you, ask whatever
> you wish, and it will be done for you. This is to my Father's
> glory, that you bear much fruit, showing yourselves to be my
> disciples. (John 15:7, 8)

Here the same promise is given in the context of remaining in Jesus, and Jesus' words remaining in the disciples. The context also includes a reference to glorifying the Father.

Earlier still, Jesus said:

> Very truly I tell you, all who have faith in me will do the works
> I have been doing, and they will do even greater things than
> these, because I am going to the Father. And I will do whatever
> you ask in my name, so that the Father may be glorified in the
> Son. You may ask me for anything in my name, and I will do
> it. (John 14:12–14)

Here it is in the context of doing similar and even greater works than Jesus and of glorifying the Father that Jesus tells the disciples, "If you ask *anything* in my name, I will do it."

We see that Jesus has repeatedly spoken about asking for anything. We expect him to be consistent of course in what he says, and so we can use details gathered from the whole conversation to give us the full context.

In summary, from our observation we can say that the promise in John 16:23 is made in the context of righteousness, the disciples bearing fruit, seeking nothing but the will of God, and glorifying the Father. This is the context in which Jesus says, "Very truly I tell you, my Father will give you *whatever* you ask in my name."

The dictionary meaning of "whatever" is "anything whatsoever". But the goal of interpretation is to go beyond the dictionary meaning to the referent. When Jesus said to his disciples, "You can ask whatever you want", "whatever" refers only to things that are righteous. Jesus is speaking in the context of disciples who are consumed with doing God's will and bearing fruit to the glory of the Father.

7

PITFALLS TO AVOID

We have repeatedly stressed how important it is to go beyond the dictionary meaning of a word to the referent. We noted, for example, that when Paul spoke of the Greeks in Romans 1:16 he was not speaking about people who were ethnically Greek (the dictionary definition), but was using the word "Greek" to refer to everyone who was not Jewish. We could determine the meaning of the word because we looked at the context.

Let us now look at some pitfalls that people sometimes fall into when interpreting the words in the Bible, and see how looking at that context helps us to avoid these pitfalls.

Pitfall 1: Root Fallacy

People fall into the root fallacy when they seek the meaning of a term by looking at the roots of the word, that is, the original words from which this word derives. For example, they might take the English word "understand" and split it up into its root components, "under" and "stand". Then they could argue that the word means to "stand under something", and build a whole interpretation on that. But that is not what the word "understand" means today.

Now it can sometimes be helpful to understand the roots. For example, the King James Version translates 1 Thessalonians 4:15 as "we which are alive and remain unto the coming of the Lord shall not *prevent* them which are asleep." What does "prevent" mean here? It may help if you know that the word "prevent" comes from two Latin words, *prae* meaning "before" and *venire* meaning "come". At the time when the KJV was being translated, this root of the word had not been forgotten (as it has been today) and so the translators of the KJV used "prevent" to mean "come before" or "precede". In the modern TNIV translation, the same verse is translated "we who are still alive, who are left till the coming of the Lord, will certainly not *precede* those who have fallen asleep."

But we would run into a problem if we used the same roots to interpret the RSV translation of Matthew 3:13–14: "Then Jesus came from Galilee to the Jordan to John, to be baptized by him. John would have *prevented* him". It would be wrong to assume that here "prevent" still means "go before". John is not saying that he wants to "precede" Jesus; he wants to stop him from doing something. This is clear from the context. John is talking about who is worthy to baptize who. The words that follow "prevent him" are, "I need to be baptized by you, and do you come to me?" So the context makes it clear that the word has to do with "not allowing", rather than "going first".

Context is more important for meaning than the word's original roots.

Pitfall 2: Semantic Anachronism

Another pitfall is assuming that the meaning a word has in the present is the same as the meaning it had in the past. The technical term for this type of error is semantic anachronism. It happens when we fail to recognize that the meaning we think of when we see a word is newer than the meaning the word had when the text was written.

Remember 1 Thessalonians 4:15 in the old King James Version: "we which are alive and remain unto the coming of the Lord shall not *prevent* them which are asleep"? A friend of mine read this and thought it weird – very weird. I can imagine him throwing away the King James Bible, thinking it has very serious theological distortions at this point.

To calm him down, I would have to ask him to do a bit more observation:

- *What* translation was he reading? The King James translation.
- *When* was this translation completed? In 1611.
- *How* long ago was that? Four hundred ago.
- *Do* languages change over a period of four hundred years? Yes.

Once he has recognized that fact, he would need to do some research to find out what "prevent" meant in the old English of four hundred years ago. He would have to consult a dictionary that gives more information about the history of the word. By looking at the dictionary and the context, he would establish that in this 1611 translation the word "prevent" meant "precede".

Just as we should not commit root fallacy and apply the old English meaning to contemporary translations, so we should not commit semantic anachronism and apply contemporary English meanings to the old translations.

> **Context includes when a book or a Bible translation was produced – the meaning of words can change over time.**

Pitfall 3: Prescriptive Fallacy

My friend who thought that the King James translation of 1 Thessalonians 4:15 was weird was also falling into another pitfall in interpretation: the prescriptive fallacy. This is the fallacy of assuming that a word has only one meaning (the one you are familiar with or the predominant meaning) and assuming that the word must mean the same thing every time it is used. So my friend assumed that the word "prevent" always means "not allow" – even though that interpretation made no sense in the context.

The prescriptive fallacy causes the problems some people find with the use of the word "justified" in Romans 3:23–24; 4:1–5; Galatians 2:16 and James 2:14–26. As we saw, this word has different meanings in Paul's letters (Romans and Galatians) and in the letter of James. Those who fail to recognize this end up being modern-day Galatians, teaching salvation by faith plus works.

A similar problem occurs with regard to the word "righteousness". In most of the places where it occurs in the New Testament, it has to do with ethical behaviour and good works. This is its meaning when Jesus tells his disciples, "Be careful not to do your 'acts of *righteousness*' in front of others, to be seen by them" (Matt 6:1). Jesus goes on to spell out what these acts are in the next verse: "when you give to the needy, do not announce it with trumpets, as the hypocrites do in the synagogues and on the streets, to be honoured by others."

Paul often uses the word "righteousness" or the adjective "righteous" to refer to behaviour or conduct. For example, in his letter to Titus he wrote that Christ "saved us, not because of deeds done by us in *righteousness*, but in virtue of his mercy" (3:5 RSV). The reference to "doing deeds" makes it clear that he is speaking about ethical behaviour.

But we would be wrong if we assumed that this is what Paul means every time he uses the word "righteousness". Look at the way he uses it in Romans 4:3–5:

> What does Scripture say? "Abraham believed God, and it was credited to him as righteousness." Now to anyone who works, their wages are not credited to them as a gift, but as an obligation. However, to anyone who does not work but trusts God who justifies the ungodly, their faith is credited as righteousness.

What do you think? Does the word "righteousness" mean ethical behaviour and good works here? No. Look at the context. Paul says that Abraham did not do good works, but is an example of an ungodly person who simply trusted in God. This becomes clear when we reread verse 5: "To anyone *who does not work but trusts* God who justifies *the ungodly*, their faith is credited as *righteousness*." As used here, righteousness has nothing to do with ethical behaviour. Rather, righteousness is the status that God gives to Abraham.

The same word can clearly have different meanings in different contexts.

Context makes it clear which of the several possible meanings of a word is intended in a particular Bible passage.

This book has already given examples of people falling into the prescriptive fallacy. That was what happened when the missionary who went back to America after years in Africa said, "I feel gay today". His hearers thought the word "gay" had only one meaning.

A variant on the prescriptive fallacy is when we read one passage and then shoot off to another passage to define a word in the first passage, while completely ignoring the context of the passages. This was what preacher Joel did when he said that in Ezra 8:21–22 (RSV) Ezra was praying for a straight way, the way of salvation. He assumed that "way" in Ezra's prayer meant exactly the same thing as it did in John 14:6, where Jesus says, "I am the *way* and the truth and the life".

This mistake would be laughable, if Joel had not been a minister of God's word for over thirty-five years. He should have known better! In his allegorizing, he ignored the context and simply shot off to another passage to interpret the word "way".

While Joel's error has no serious doctrinal implications, this is not always the case. I have heard someone of considerable standing in ministry present an exposition of James 2:14–26. When he came to verse 21, where it says, "Was not Abraham our father justified by works, when he offered his son Isaac upon the altar?" (RSV), the expositor shot off to Romans 4:1–5 to find the meaning of the word "justify" and claimed to have evidence that James taught salvation by faith plus works!

Because context determines the meaning of a passage or term, you must not simply shoot off to other passages where the same word is used and ignore the context of the word you are reading.

It is true that sometimes the context may not give much help in determining the exact meaning of a passage or term. So at times we do need to consult other passages that give more details. But when you do this, you must be careful to ensure that the other passages are parallel passages – that is, that the context is similar to that of the passage you are looking at.

For example, look at the word "justify" in Galatians 2:15–16:

> We who are Jews by birth and not sinful Gentiles know that a person is not justified by observing the law, but by faith in Jesus Christ. So we, too, have put our faith in Christ Jesus that we may be justified by faith in Christ and not by observing the law, because by observing the law no one will be justified.

If you are seeking the meaning of the word "justify" in this passage, you can go to Romans 4:1–4 to get help. The context there is similar to that of Galatians. In Galatians 2:15–16 Paul is speaking about being justified by faith rather than works, and he is dealing with the same topic in Romans 4:1–4. Thus, the contexts parallel each other. What Paul says in Romans is:

> What then shall we say that Abraham, the forefather of us Jews, discovered in this matter? If, in fact, Abraham was justified by works, he had something to boast about – but not before God. What does Scripture say? "Abraham believed God, and it was credited to him as righteousness."

> Now to anyone who works, their wages are not credited to them as a gift, but as an obligation. However, to anyone who does not work but trusts [believes] God who justifies the ungodly, their faith is credited as righteousness.

This passage spells out that in Abraham's case being justified meant being credited with righteousness or having righteousness accorded to him or being declared righteous.

By contrast, in James 2:14–26, James is talking about believers who are not living out their faith. That is a very different context, and so we cannot consult it to determine what the word "justify" means in Galatians 2:15–16.

Remember, then, to avoid the pitfall of reading one passage and shooting off to another passage to define a term without paying any attention to the context in which the terms are used.

Pitfall 4: Totality Transfer

The final pitfall in interpretation we will consider is called "totality transfer". This is what happens when we assume that a word carries all its various meanings whenever it is used.

I was once attending a Bible study where the leader told us to open our Bibles to Hebrews 11:1: "Now faith is being sure of what we hope for and certain of what we do not see." He then asked the question, "What does the word *faith* mean?" His answer was, "Faith means belief, faithfulness, reliability, trust, confidence, firm persuasion, assurance or firm conviction." I waited to hear which of these meanings applied when it came to the use of the word "faith" in Hebrews 11:1. My friends, I waited in vain!

The pitfall this teacher fell into was totality transfer. When you give an answer that is as broad as his was, you have not explained the meaning of the passage or term in a particular passage. Your audience will be left bewildered and frustrated.

A word does not carry all of its possible meanings in any one context.

8

TWO TYPES OF CONTEXT

We now know the first and fundamental principle of interpretation: context determines the meaning of a passage or term. But there are two types of context and it is important that we look at both. There is the literary context, that is, the words that have been written down as part of a book or letter. We will return to this later. There is also the historical context, which includes the physical, geographical, cultural and ideological context of the authors and the people to whom they wrote, as well as the historical events being referred to.

Historical Context

The historical context helps shed light on the meaning of a passage or term. To see how it does this, let's look again at Romans 1:16, where Paul says, "For I am not ashamed of the gospel: it is the power of God for salvation to everyone who has faith, to the Jew first and also to the *Greek*" (RSV). When we interpret these words, it helps to know that in Paul's day many Jews categorized everyone in the world as either Jewish or not-Jewish, and lumped all the non-Jews together in the category labelled "Greek". So, when Paul says that the gospel "is the power of God for salvation to everyone who has faith, to the Jew first and also to the Greek," he is not saying that salvation is limited to ethnic Jews and

Greeks. What he means is that the gospel is for *everyone*. Knowing the historical context sheds light on the meaning of this passage.

Another example is the story of the Good Samaritan in Luke 10:25–37. In introducing this story, Luke says, "On one occasion an expert in the law stood up to test Jesus. 'Teacher', he asked, 'what must I do to inherit eternal life?'" (10:25). We observe that this lawyer's motive was not to learn but to test Jesus.

As they talked, the matter of loving your neighbour came up: "But he wanted to justify himself, so he asked Jesus, 'And who is my neighbour?'" (10:29). Again, we observe that his motive was not to learn but to justify himself.

So we have identified the person Jesus was talking to as someone who was out to test Jesus and justify himself. He was not someone who was eager to learn, the type of person for whom you only need to touch on a subject and he will get the point. All this lawyer wanted was a theoretical debate about how one identified one's neighbours. However, Jesus was not about theoretical discourse and debate but about turning people around and calling them to personal devotion to God and his word. This lawyer needed something that would affect not only his head but also his heart. So Jesus told the story of the Good Samaritan:

> A man was going down from Jerusalem to Jericho, when he fell into the hands of robbers. They stripped him of his clothes, beat him and went away, leaving him half dead. A priest happened to be going down the same road, and when he saw the man, he passed by on the other side. So too, a Levite, when he came to the place and saw him, passed by on the other side. But a Samaritan, as he traveled, came where the man was; and when he saw him, he took pity on him. He went to him and bandaged his wounds, pouring on oil and wine. Then he put the man on his own donkey, brought him to an inn and took care of him. The next day he took out two denarii and gave them to the innkeeper. 'Look after him', he said, 'and when I return, I will reimburse you for any extra expense you may have.'
>
> "Which of these three do you think was a neighbour to the man who fell into the hands of robbers?"

The expert in the law replied, "The one who had mercy on him." Jesus told him, "Go and do likewise." (Luke 10:30–37)

Jesus turned the lawyer's question around. He changed the question from "Who is my neighbour?" to "Am I a neighbour?" That is the important question! The issue is not a topic for theoretical discussion but a challenge to live in a way that shows personal devotion to God.

Jesus presented this challenge in a way that was pointed and penetrating. He used a Samaritan as his hero! This lawyer was a Jew. How did Jews and Samaritans get on in those days? This question calls for investigation of the historical context.

The answer you will find is that there was deep animosity between the Jews and the Samaritans. We see this in Luke 9:51–53, which describes how some Samaritans refused to receive Jesus: "He sent messengers on ahead, who went into a Samaritan village to get things ready for him; but the people there did not welcome him, because he was heading for Jerusalem." The Samaritans' attitude made James and John so angry that they wanted Jesus "to call fire down from heaven to destroy them" (Luke 9:54).

The Jews, in turn, despised the Samaritans. The Jews knew God; the Samaritans did not – that was the thinking. And it was true that Samaritan worship was not wholesome. Do you remember Jesus' conversation with the Samaritan woman at the well? He told her, "You Samaritans worship what you do not know; we worship what we do know, for salvation is from the Jews" (John 4:22).

Given this historical background, you can understand how the story of the Good Samaritan shocked and challenged the Jewish lawyer. What the priest and Levite, key representatives of Jewish piety, failed to do, a Samaritan did, proving himself a neighbour to someone in need.

To get the same effect today, we might want to think of a bishop and a terrorist. We expect bishops to help people and are not surprised when they do. But if a bishop refused to help someone and a terrorist went out of his way to help – that would be a shock and a challenge to those who think themselves godly!

Understanding the historical background helps us to understand the challenge Jesus is presenting to the lawyer when he changes the question to "Am I a neighbour like this Good Samaritan?" The historical background brings this challenge into sharp focus.

The historical context augments the literary context to bring out the meaning of a passage or word.

For another example, let us look at 1 Timothy 5:23. I once happened upon a friend who was heavily drunk. As soon as he saw me, he tried to justify his condition, saying, "You know, Bishop, the Bible says you should drink a little wine."

It is interesting that people who use 1 Timothy 5:23 to justify their love of alcohol never quote the verse in full. What it actually says is, "Stop drinking only water, and use a little wine because of your stomach and your frequent illnesses."

Paul's reference to Timothy's "stomach and your frequent illnesses" makes it clear that in 1 Timothy he is speaking about the use of wine for medicinal purposes. From our knowledge of the historical background, we know that this was common at the time. We have just read how the Good Samaritan cared for the wounded man by pouring oil and wine on his wounds (Luke 10:34). So when Paul tells Timothy to drink some wine, he is not speaking about drinking simply for pleasure. Once again, the historical context augments the literary context to bring out the meaning.

However, although the historical context is important and helpful in shedding light on the meaning of a passage or term, it does not always provide the final answer about the meaning of every term. An author can expand the meaning of a word. For example, let's look at the term "word", or *logos* in Greek, in John's Gospel. John says:

> In the beginning was the Word, and the Word was with God,
> and the Word was God ... The Word became flesh and made
> his dwelling among us ... full of grace and truth. (1:1, 14)

To the Greeks, "the Word", or *logos*, was the ultimate impersonal force or reason that controlled the universe. In John's Gospel, however, the

Word is personal. John talks of the Word as being "with God" and as being God.

Moreover, in Greek thinking the things above (that is, heavenly things) were holy and completely separate from the things below (earthly things). All earthly things, including matter, were considered evil. The things above would never come into contact with earthly things because they were evil. But the Word came in contact with matter through the incarnation. The very idea would be quite unthinkable to Greeks: the Word became flesh!

Here we can see how John took a familiar term, one with a specific meaning in his historical context, and used it to establish a connection with the people he was writing to. But he did not leave the term unchanged; he sharpened its meaning and applied it to Jesus Christ, the God-man.

Literary Context

Having considered the historical context we need to return to the literary context. The literary context includes the words of the verse itself, and progressively moves outwards to include the chapter in which the verse appears, the book in which that chapter appears, other books by the same author, other books in the same Testament and, ultimately, the rest of the Bible. The doctrine shaped by the whole Bible also affects our understanding of what we read. But our interpretation should always start with close observation and interpretation of the text itself in its immediate context! The immediate context is primary.[11]

It is important to note that the literary context takes precedence over the historical context when it comes to determining the meaning of a passage or term. To understand this point, let's look at the way the term "Son of God" is used in John's Gospel. In the historical context, "son of God" was used to refer to a supernatural being and did not indicate that the being was equal with God. Even in Job 1:6 (KJV) the "sons of God" are no more than supernatural beings, without any implication that they are equal with God. So background study may allow for an understanding of the title "Son of God" that does not imply equality with God.

However, in the literary context of John's Gospel, that is, in terms of what is written in the book of John, the term "Son of God" does signify "equality with God". How do we know this? Look at this portion of John's Gospel:

> The man went away and told the Jewish leaders that it was Jesus who had made him well. So, because Jesus was doing these things on the Sabbath, the Jewish leaders began to persecute him. In his defense Jesus said to them, "My Father is always at his work to this very day, and I too am working." For this reason they tried all the more to kill him; not only was he breaking the Sabbath, but he was even calling God his own Father, making himself equal with God.
>
> Jesus gave them this answer: "Very truly I tell you, the Son can do nothing by himself; he can do only what he sees his Father doing, because whatever the Father does the Son also does." (John 5:15–19)

Remember, earlier we said that interpretation involves determining what the author meant. Here, John himself comments on Jesus being the "Son of God" and says, "he was even calling God his own Father, making himself equal with God" (5:18).

These words from the literary context firmly establish that when used of Jesus, "Son of God" implies "equality with God". We can use these words to refute the argument heard in some circles that in John's Gospel Jesus is merely a son of God and not equal with God.

The historical context sheds light on the meaning of a passage or term, but does not determine its meaning. The literary context is more important.

Overall, then, context determines the meaning of a passage or term. This statement should, however, be balanced by the reminder that Scripture does not contradict Scripture, because Scripture is inspired by

God and is inerrant. If your interpretation of a passage contradicts other Scriptures, it is wise to revisit your interpretation more carefully.

When this happens, you should consult other people and other books. You may have to fight the temptation of wanting to be original and impressive. If you are a preacher, you may want people to say after your sermon, "That was impressive; I have never heard that interpretation before. That was original; the man is good!" Do not succumb to this temptation; it has led many astray. Consult others. But remember to stay firmly rooted in context. Context should be your sweet song in interpretation, because context determines the meaning of a passage or a word. Context is that critical.

Practise Engaging with the Context

It is amazing, and actually sad, how often context is overlooked, not just by simple folks but even by teachers and preachers, people who should know better. I remember watching a preacher on television. He had an audience of thousands, and the people were hanging onto his every word. But he completely ignored context. It seemed that to him Scripture consists of words and phrases dangling on individual threads from heaven, without any context at all. And there are many preachers like him! They take that word, or this phrase, and run with it wherever they want.

The preacher on television read from Revelation 3:8: "See, I have placed before you an open door" and he used that verse to work the crowd to a frenzy: "Do you want to get rich? God says 'I have placed before you an open door!' Are your finances not enough and are you desperately seeking a way out? God says, 'I have placed before you an open door.' The possibilities are all around you; the sky is not even the limit, for God says, 'I have placed before you an open door'." To this preacher, the "open door" was all about unending possibilities for wealth and a problem-free life in the present.

Now, let us read about this "open door" in its context, which is Revelation 3:7–9:

To the angel of the church in Philadelphia write:

These are the words of him who is holy and true, who holds the key of David. What he opens no one can shut, and what he shuts no one can open. I know your deeds. See, I have placed before you an open door that no one can shut. I know that you have little strength, yet you have kept my word and have not denied my name. I will make those who are of the synagogue of Satan, who claim to be Jews though they are not, but are liars – I will make them come and fall down at your feet and acknowledge that I have loved you.

The situation in Philadelphia was that the Jews there were being unfaithful to their calling as God's people. They were persecuting the church. So Christ encourages the church by telling them, "I will make those who are of the synagogue of Satan, who claim to be Jews though they are not, but are liars – I will make them come and fall down at your feet and acknowledge that I have loved you." God basically disowns this group of Jews.

So this is the context in which we ask the question, "What is this 'open door'?" Is there anything else in this passage that sheds some light on what it means? Well, there is the statement that the one who opens and shuts the door is the Holy One, the True One, who holds "the key of David". What this person "opens no one can shut, and what he shuts no one can open." But what is this "key of David"? The cross-references in our Bible point us to Isaiah 22:22.

When we find an allusion to the Old Testament, we should go and study the context of the Old Testament passage that is being quoted or alluded to. We will then understand the link between the two passages.

Let's look at Isaiah 22:15–22 to get the context. It reads:

This is what the Lord, the LORD Almighty, says:

"Go, say to this steward,
    to Shebna, who is in charge of the palace:
What are you doing here and who gave you permission
    to cut out a grave for yourself here,
hewing your grave on the height
    and chiseling your resting place in the rock?

Beware, the LORD is about to take firm hold of you
   and hurl you away, you mighty man.
He will roll you up tightly like a ball
   and throw you into a large country.
There you will die
   and there the chariots you were so proud of
   will become a disgrace to your master's house.
I will depose you from your office,
   and you will be ousted from your position.

In that day I will summon my servant, Eliakim son of Hilkiah.
I will clothe him with your robe and fasten your sash around
him and hand your authority over to him. He will be a father
to those who live in Jerusalem and to the house of Judah. I will
place on his shoulder the key to the house of David; what he
opens no one can shut, and what he shuts no one can open."

This prophecy is addressed to a steward called Shebna, who had turned
out to be unfaithful. He was behaving as if his master's palace belonged
to him. He had even made a tomb for himself in his master's property.
God was saying that he would remove Shebna from his position of
authority and give authority over the household to another man, called
Eliakim. Eliakim will then hold "the key to the house of David".

Do you see how this passage parallels the one in Revelations 3:7–9?
Just as Shebna was unfaithful, so the Jews who are persecuting the church
at Philadelphia are being unfaithful. So God disowns them and gives the
key of David to one who is "holy and true". The key has been given to
the one who should have it. The appointment of Eliakim prefigures the
appointment of Jesus, the Davidic Messiah who is perfectly holy and true
and who has been given the key of David, which in its final fulfilment is
the key to the messianic kingdom. He has absolute authority over entry
into that kingdom. When he opens its doors, no one shall shut them;
when he shuts them, no one shall open them.

So what is happening in Revelation 3:7–9 is that the one who has
absolute authority over the kingdom is comforting and reassuring the
church at Philadelphia. What he is saying could be put like this, "The
Jews of the synagogue may be against you, but those Jews are disowned

– they are of the synagogue of Satan. The true one with authority, absolute authority, has let you, the true believers, into the kingdom – he has set before you an open door."

So the open door is not about escaping poverty and getting rich now. It is about spiritual salvation. That preacher on television was way off the mark, and it was all because he did not bother to engage with the context. He treated the words of Scripture as if they exist in isolation. But it is context that determines the meaning of a passage or a word. That is the cardinal principle of interpretation.

9

THE HARMONY OF SCRIPTURE

Scripture does not contradict Scripture. Put positively, Scripture is in harmony with Scripture. This is the second principle of interpretation that we will discuss in this book. Because Scripture is in harmony with itself, our interpretation of a passage or term should not contradict any other passage.

However, when you are reading the Bible, you may suddenly come across verses in Scripture that seem to contradict other verses. If this happens to you, stop and look again. Look again and look even harder. Read the surrounding verses, consult other believers, look up what commentaries have to say. You may be missing some important information that would affect your interpretation.

Look Again

The principle that Scripture is in harmony with Scripture keeps us in check when we do interpretation so that we do not wander off into doctrinal errors. Let's start by looking at a simple, straightforward case: I was once challenged by someone who insisted, "There is a passage in the Gospels that contradicts Paul's teaching of salvation by faith alone, apart from works." When I asked him which one, he referred me to the story of Zacchaeus:

> Zacchaeus stood up and said to the Lord, "Look, Lord! Here and now I give half of my possessions to the poor, and if I have cheated anybody out of anything, I will pay back four times the amount."
>
> Jesus said to him, "Today salvation has come to this house, because this man, too, is a son of Abraham. For the Son of Man came to seek and to save what was lost." (Luke 19:8–10)

Now, it might look as if this passage teaches salvation by works, but have you looked hard? Please, look harder. Is Zacchaeus saved because he gives away his possessions, or is his new generosity evidence of the fact that he has been saved? Zacchaeus believed, and his faith showed – it became evident in his works. Salvation is by faith alone, as Paul teaches (Gal 2:15–16). But this faith is not dead faith; it prompts us to do good works (Jas 2:14–26) because faith in Christ transforms us: "If anyone is in Christ, he is a new creation; the old has passed away, behold, the new has come" (2 Cor 5:17). Zacchaeus' behaviour is an example of this transformation. His story in no way contradicts the scriptural teaching that we are saved by faith apart from works.

If you think you see disharmony in Scripture, look again – you may be missing something important.

On another occasion I was teaching a seminar on the basics of the gospel. I stressed that Scripture teaches that people need to believe in Christ personally for salvation. We looked at several passages of Scripture that confirmed this point, including John 3:16–18:

> For God so loved the world that he gave his one and only Son, that whoever believes in him shall not perish but have eternal life. For God did not send his Son into the world to condemn the world, but to save the world through him. Whoever believes in him is not condemned, but whoever does not believe stands condemned already because they have not believed in the name of God's one and only Son.

This passage teaches that the individual who believes has eternal life and the individual who does not believe is condemned. This is tight. It leaves no room for any other way: one must believe personally in order to be saved.

However, one of the participants in the seminar raised his hand and said, "Sir, in Acts 16:31 an individual believed on behalf of others. There Paul says to the Philippian jailer, 'Believe in the Lord Jesus, and you will be saved – you and your household'."

As you know by now, when someone quotes a verse, you should always remember to look at it in its full context. When you read the entire passage some details may emerge that shed light on the issue. So we read the whole passage, from verse 29 to 31:

> The jailer called for lights, rushed in and fell trembling before Paul and Silas. He then brought them out and asked, "Sirs, what must I do to be saved?"
> They replied, "Believe in the Lord Jesus, and you will be saved – you and your household." Then they spoke the word of the Lord to him and to all the others in his house. At that hour of the night the jailer took them and washed their wounds; then immediately he and all his household were baptized.

I asked, "Have you looked hard at this whole passage?" He said, "Yes, Sir." "Then," I said, "Let us look even harder."

We agreed that Paul's words could mean either "Believe in the Lord Jesus and both you and your household will be saved" or "Believe in the Lord Jesus and you will be saved. And if your household do the same, they too will be saved."

Then we looked carefully at what happened in the next verse. It says that Paul and Silas preached the gospel not only to the jailer, but also to everyone in his family. And the following verse says that after hearing this preaching, the jailer and all the members of his household were baptized. That "all" is significant. It was not just the jailer alone who believed and was baptized; all those in his household did the same.

Then I asked my friend whether he thought that Paul's words to the jailer should be interpreted as meaning, "Believe in the Lord Jesus and both you and your household will be saved" or "Believe in the Lord

Jesus and you will be saved. And if your household do the same, they too will be saved." He answered, "The second interpretation is better because it seems Paul and Silas thought it necessary to preach the gospel not only to the jailer but also to the whole household. And these people were only baptized after they had heard the gospel." I said to him, "Good answer."

Sometimes, like my friend, we are too quick to see disharmony and contradiction in Scripture where it does not exist. Always remember that if Scripture seems to contradict itself, look again. Look again, and look even harder. Perhaps there is an angle that you might be missing. Look again at the passage and the context because Scripture is in harmony with Scripture.

Look Deeper

The apparent contradictions we have looked at so far are fairly simple to resolve. But sometimes we encounter more difficult issues. For example, in Leviticus 11 animals such as camels, hares and pigs are labelled as unclean, and God's people are forbidden to eat them. But in the New Testament, Jesus declares all foods "clean":

> Don't you see that nothing that enters you from the outside can defile you? For it doesn't go into your heart but into your stomach, and then out of your body. (In saying this, Jesus declared all foods clean.) (Mark 7:18–19)

You might ask, "Isn't this a case of the New Testament contradicting the Old Testament?"

When we encounter passages like this, there is another very important principle we should consider. This principle is called progressive revelation. God sometimes chose to reveal only part of his truth at one period of history, and then explained the same idea later in more detail, from a different perspective. That is what is happening in the passage quoted above. The more restrictive Old Testament teaching about food was meant as an object lesson to teach God's people about the importance of purity and honouring him in all aspects of life. Jesus supplemented the earlier revelation by pointing out that what really makes us unclean is the evil in our hearts. The Old Testament teaching stood until it was supplemented by Jesus' teaching in the New Testament. We can now eat whatever we want as a matter of doctrine, though we should not be unmindful of our health.

> When later passages appear to contradict earlier ones, it may be because God has revealed more of his truth to later generations. We need to take into account the possibility of progressive revelation.

Beware of Pre-understandings

In an earlier chapter, we spoke about some pitfalls that we can fall into. But there is still another one that we need to discuss, as it too can endanger your interpretation. This pitfall is pre-understandings, that is, the understandings (or preconceptions) that we bring with us when we read a passage. Our knowledge of traditional interpretations of a text, or of the theology of our church or denomination, or our cultural or philosophical biases can all influence our interpretation.

None of us is free of pre-understandings. I remember one particular occasion when I myself fell into the trap of paying more attention to my own pre-understanding than to what Scripture was actually saying. Many years ago I attended a seminar on salvation. The teacher told us to turn to John 6:37–44 where Jesus says,

> All whom the Father gives me will come to me, and whoever comes to me I will never drive away. For I have come down from heaven not to do my will but to do the will of him who sent me. And this is the will of him who sent me, that I shall lose none of all those he has given me, but raise them up at the last day ... No one can come to me unless the Father who sent me draws them, and I will raise them up at the last day.

The teacher told us that when we come to Jesus, there is no question of our being lost again; we are eternally secure because Jesus will never lose us.

The moment the teacher mentioned eternal security, I switched off. I was looking at him, but I was not listening. He could explain that text as long as he liked, but I was not going to listen to his arguments! I dismissed everything he had to say. I was thinking thoughts like "Which denomination does he belong to? Oh – *that* one. Well, they may believe such things, but we don't!" I allowed my pre-understanding about eternal security (derived from my own denominational background) to prevent me from listening to the text and thinking about what it said. With this mindset, I could not interact with the text and learn from it and from the teacher.

We all have pre-understanding. However, being aware of this problem will help us to watch out for situations where we are imposing our own interpretation on a text, without caring about what the text itself actually says.

If we do not keep our pre-understandings in check, they can endanger our interpretation.

10

APPLICATION AND CONTEXT

Application is the logical and necessary step after interpretation. It is how we put God's word into effect, showing how what we believe affects the way we walk with God in our lives and ministries. The need to do this is clear from Paul's words to Timothy:

> All Scripture is God-breathed and is useful for teaching, rebuking, correcting and training in righteousness, so that all God's people may be thoroughly equipped for every good work. (2 Tim 3:16–17)

Proper application must be based on proper interpretation. And to make a proper application, the context that an interpretation is applied to today must be comparable to the context of the passage being interpreted. In other words, you must connect with a passage in a way that is consistent with its context and meaning.

Let's begin with an everyday example: During an election in my country, I was in a village, and I overheard two residents arguing. One insisted, "We ordinary people only get one vote; I bet the president has more!" "Don't be so stupid," the other replied. "In elections it doesn't matter if you are a president or a villager, ordinary or special, rich or poor; we are all equal as citizens."

Do you think that someone could interpret this statement that "we are all equal as citizens" to mean that any citizen of Uganda could give orders to the Ugandan army or police force, or sign a parliamentary bill into law? That would be a wrong application. The right to do those things is reserved for the person occupying a particular position. Only the president can exercise presidential authority, despite the fact that at election time, all citizens are equal. Most of us would not even begin to think otherwise.

Yet preachers often make the same sort of mistake when they take truths that apply in one context and apply them in a very different context. Here are some examples of how this is sometimes done.

Overspiritualization

A preacher asked his audience to turn to Luke 2:43–45, which he then read,

> After the Festival was over, while his parents were returning home, the boy Jesus stayed behind in Jerusalem, but they were unaware of it. Thinking he was in their company, they travelled on for a day. Then they began looking for him among their relatives and friends. When they did not find him, they went back to Jerusalem to look for him.

From this passage, the preacher drew an application and said, "We should not be left behind in our spiritual walk!"

The person who was with me was puzzled, "Where on earth did he get that? Is that an allegorical application?" You probably also noted the lack of connection immediately. This application does not connect with the context of the passage. Jesus' family left him behind on their literal journey, but the preacher turned this literal journey into a spiritual journey.

This example may be extreme, but it brings the importance of context into sharp focus. In fact, let me make my point again because we often overlook it! The context that a passage is applied to must be comparable to the context of the original passage.

Mistaken Identity

Remember the young man I mentioned in chapter 3? He was in financial distress and interpreted Psalm 2:8 as a promise that God would give him the ends of the earth as his possession. But that promise was given in the context of God rebuking the kings of the earth and the rulers who "band together against the LORD and against his anointed" (Ps 2:2). The promise was given directly to the "anointed", the Davidic king and Messiah (Ps 2:7–8). He is the one who says,

> I will proclaim the Lord's decree:
> He said to me, "You are my son; today I have become your father.
> Ask me, and I will make the nations your inheritance, the ends of the earth your possession.
> You will break them with a rod of iron; you will dash them to pieces like pottery."

The young man made a mistake in applying this promise to his own life. However, he could have been comforted by the knowledge that the Messiah, our Lord, possesses all things, even the ends of the earth. We are in God's hands, and what is this little financial problem to him? That would have been okay, but it was not okay for the man to claim this promise directly for himself.

> **The context that a passage is applied to today must be comparable to the context of the original passage.**

If you are a believer, you can apply this passage to your life in the same way, because the Messiah is your Lord and has the ability to provide for you too. This application is consistent with the context of this passage: you have not claimed the possession of the ends of the earth for yourself, but you have claimed the one who possesses the ends of the earth as your provider.

A straightforward example of comparable contexts is Psalm 23:1, "The LORD is my Shepherd". The psalmist is speaking simply as a believer. I, too, am a believer. I am in the same category as the psalmist, so I fit the context of the psalm. Therefore, I can also take comfort that the LORD is my Shepherd.

Shaky Contexts

Another example I want to touch on is the much-loved verse, "My God will meet all your needs according to the riches of his glory in Christ Jesus" (Phil 4:19). This is a verse that Christians turn to when they fall on hard times. Paul wrote it in the context of comforting the believers at Philippi who were in financial need. So, if you are a Christian and are in financial need you could say, "I fit the category; I fit the context."

But before you assume that you are in exactly the same position as the Philippian believers, let's find out a little more about them. Paul had arrived in Philippi during his second missionary journey. There he met Lydia, who after being baptized invited Paul, Timothy and Silas to stay at her home (Acts 16:14–15). Philippi was also the home of the jailer who took Paul and Silas into his house and "set a meal before them" (Acts 16:33–34). This generosity continued: the Philippian believers supported Paul in his ministry by giving, again and again, even when Paul had moved on to minister in other places. They kept giving although they were themselves poor.

We know about this ongoing generosity because when Paul writes to the Corinthians he specifically mentions the churches of Macedonia, the area where Philippi was a leading city (Acts 16:11–12).

> And now, brothers and sisters, we want you to know about the grace that God has given the Macedonian churches. In the midst of a very severe trial, their overflowing joy and their extreme poverty welled up in rich generosity. For I testify that they gave as much as they were able, and even beyond their ability. (2 Cor 8:1–3)

Later in the same letter, Paul tells the Corinthians,

> I robbed other churches by receiving support from them so as to serve you. And when I was with you and needed something,

I was not a burden to anyone, for the brothers and sisters who
came from Macedonia supplied what I needed. (2 Cor 11:8–9)

At the beginning of his letter to the Philippians, Paul commended them:

I thank my God every time I remember you. In all my prayers
for all of you, I always pray with joy because of your partnership
in the gospel from the first day until now. (Phil 1:3–5)

Later on in chapter 4, from which our verse comes, Paul again commends
them:

Yet it was good of you to share in my troubles. Moreover, as
you Philippians know, in the early days of your acquaintance
with the gospel, when I set out from Macedonia, not one
church shared with me in the matter of giving and receiving,
except you only; for even when I was in Thessalonica, you
sent me aid more than once when I was in need ... I have
received full payment and have more than enough. I am amply
supplied, now that I have received from Epaphroditus the gifts
you sent. They are a fragrant offering, an acceptable sacrifice,
pleasing to God. (Phil 4:14–18)

It is in light of all this generosity and sacrificial giving by the Philippians
that Paul encourages them saying, "My God will meet all your needs
according to the riches of his glory in Christ Jesus" (Phil 4:19).

Now, do you fit in the same category as the Philippian believers? Are
you in a similar context? Or are you inclined to be mean with money and
focused on your own comforts rather than on others and God's work?
If the latter, can you still turn to Philippians 4:19 when hard times come
your way?

Our God is good despite our failings, and we can turn to him –
always. We are encouraged to "cast all your anxiety on him because he
cares for you" (1 Pet 5:7). But perhaps Philippians 4:19 is not the verse
we should use when seeking to claim God's promises if we have been
mean and selfish.

Practise Application

Before leaving this chapter, I want to challenge you to apply all that you have learned to interpreting Galatians 3:28. Let me quote that verse in its context:

> Before the coming of this faith, we were held in custody under the law, locked up until the faith that was to come would be revealed. So the law was put in charge of us until Christ came that we might be justified by faith. Now that this faith has come, we are no longer under the supervision of the law.
>
> So in Christ Jesus you are all children of God through faith, for all of you who were baptized into Christ have clothed yourselves with Christ. There is neither Jew nor Gentile, neither slave nor free, neither male nor female, for you are all one in Christ Jesus. If you belong to Christ, then you are Abraham's seed, and heirs according to the promise. (Gal 3:23–29)

Now focus on verse 28: "There is neither Jew nor Gentile, neither slave nor free, neither male nor female, for you are all one in Christ Jesus." This verse is often quoted in discussions about whether women can be ordained or serve in positions of leadership. But what does it actually say? How should we interpret it? Does it mean that there is absolutely no distinction between men and women?

To answer this question, you need to study the context. Is Paul talking about salvation (and specifically about how we are saved) or is he talking about believers' roles in ministry, or about something else?

You probably already have your own views about the role of women in the church and the interpretation of this verse. But do you remember what was said about pre-understanding at the end of the last chapter? You might need to remind yourself of it now, before you set out to interpret this verse!

Finally, remember that for proper application, the context in which you apply a passage to today must be compatible with the original meaning and context of the passage.

I have raised this question about Galatians 3:28 because I want you to practise interpreting and applying Scripture without bias, even when dealing with a controversial subject. (And do not forget that this verse is not the only one that applies to the issue of women's ordination, so that interpreting it correctly will not settle the issue – although it will throw light on the argument.)

11

APPLICATION AND THE HARMONY OF SCRIPTURE

I am a Ugandan, but I lived and worked in Kenya for a number of years. My family and I loved going home to Uganda whenever we had the opportunity. We were always very excited about going, and even the children looked forward to the long road trip.

We would usually wake up very early in the morning and hit the road by 5:00 a.m. At 8:00 a.m. we would stop to have breakfast in Nakuru, a town in western Kenya. An hour later we would set off again, driving through Kericho and on to Kisumu. We would reach Kisumu around noon and have lunch at the Wimpy restaurant there. This lunch was the highlight of the road trip for our kids; they loved the hamburgers, French fries and ice cream cones! We would leave Kisumu by 1:00 p.m., and two hours later we would reach the border town of Busia and cross into our beloved Uganda.

I remember one particular trip very well. As we prepared to set out, our neighbour overheard the noise and wandered over. "So, you're heading out through Nakuru and to Kisumu, are you? You must be going to Uganda." "Oh yes," I said. "And as you can tell, we are really excited to be going!"

We left Nairobi an hour earlier than usual so that we would reach Uganda earlier. Everything went smoothly, and as we approached

Kisumu, the children were singing in the back seat. Suddenly I found I could not change gears! The clutch cable of my Fiat had broken. "Well," I thought, "I am in gear and provided I don't stop or slow down, I should be able to reach a garage where there is a mechanic who can fix things." Those who have driven in Africa know how optimistic such thinking is. The next thing I saw was a police roadblock! But miraculously the police waved me past and the traffic was light. We made it to the first petrol station in Kisumu.

I climbed out and asked whether there was a mechanic there who could fix my clutch. "Yes, we have someone who specializes in working on Fiats." I was delighted. By 11:00 a.m. the mechanic was working on the car. He was still working on it at noon, at 2 p.m., at 3 p.m. ... Seven hours later, and he was still at it. And this was a "Fiat specialist"! (Be careful that you, too, do not claim to know what you are doing when you actually don't, or you will end up frustrating yourself and those you try to help.)

Someone came up to me and said, "You know, there's another mechanic who can fix your car." So we towed my vehicle to another garage, and within thirty minutes the mechanic there had installed a new clutch cable. He cheerfully remarked, "Actually, this should have taken me fifteen minutes, but I had to fix some things that the first mechanic damaged."

All our plans for an early arrival in Uganda were thwarted. It was 9:00 p.m. before we crossed the border.

Confusing Prescription and Description

Now, suppose that two thousand years from now someone were to teach a lesson about travel from Kenya to Uganda by road and used my story as the authoritative reference. Suppose that teacher said, "The *only* way to go from Nairobi, Kenya, to Uganda by road was to go via Nakuru, Kericho and Kisumu and on to the border town of Busia." The teacher would be wrong! There are many different ways one can travel to Uganda. This teacher would be turning "what happened" into "what had to happen".

My story was about how my family chose to travel to Uganda. My purpose was not to elaborate on the ways one could travel from Nairobi to Uganda by road, so I did not mention any other routes. I did not even bother to say why I went through Kisumu. I was simply telling you what route we took.

If the teacher wanted detailed information on how people used to travel from Nairobi to Uganda by road, he could start with my story, but he would also need to consult other sources on the subject. Maps and guidebooks would suggest a number of other routes. Consulting as many of these sources as possible would give a far fuller picture of the options. The teacher would then not teach it as prescriptive (that is, what must be done to travel to Uganda) but rather as descriptive (that is, what happened in my case), describing the route I used to take as just one of the possible routes to Uganda.

Our interpretation of Scripture often runs into trouble when we make the same mistake as the teacher and treat passages of Scripture that describe what happened as if they were prescriptions telling us what must happen. When we do this, we can end up violating the principle that Scripture is in harmony with itself.

Do not turn the "descriptive" (what happened) into the "prescriptive" (what must happen) without considering other passages on a subject.

The story of Zacchaeus in Luke 19:8–9 illustrates the problem well:

> Zacchaeus stood up and said to the Lord, "Look, Lord! Here and now I give half of my possessions to the poor, and if I have cheated anybody out of anything, I will pay back four times the amount."
>
> Jesus said to him, "Today salvation has come to this house, because this man, too, is a son of Abraham." (Luke 19:8–9)

Suppose someone used these verses to teach on how believers should give and insisted that believers in Christ ought to give half of their goods to the poor. This teacher would be wrong, turning what happened in

Zacchaeus' case into what ought to happen in all cases. He or she would be confusing what is descriptive and what is prescriptive.

If you want to teach believers how they should give, make sure that you consider the whole teaching of Scripture on this matter. Pay careful attention to the passages that teach on giving as such. One example is 2 Corinthians 9:6–7:

> Whoever sows sparingly will also reap sparingly, and whoever sows generously will also reap generously. Each of you should give what you have decided in your heart to give, not reluctantly or under compulsion, for God loves a cheerful giver.

This passage teaches believers to give and to give generously, not reluctantly or because they feel that they must, but cheerfully and freely, for that is what pleases God. That is how Zacchaeus gave. He did not give with an agenda, hoping to reap benefits later. To give that way is to give out of fear of missing out on some blessing or not receiving God's help when we are in trouble. Zacchaeus' only agenda was to please God.

Rather than taking the specifics of what happened in the story of Zacchaeus as indicating what must happen in every Christian's life, we can apply the principles underlying his actions that are in line with the whole teaching of Scripture on giving. This approach upholds the harmony of Scripture and avoids making applications that are not in harmony with the rest of Scripture. Our responsibility is to give, and to give cheerfully, and to leave the matter of rewards for giving in God's hands.

You might want to bear the difference between description and prescription in mind when thinking about controversial issues such as the Holy Spirit and speaking in tongues. In light of what has been said here, how are you going to interpret and apply verses in the book of Acts and the teaching of 1 Corinthians 12?

I am not going to get into a discussion of that specific issue in this book, because my intention is simply to get you to apply the principles of interpretation you have learned.

I will now turn to discuss three other areas where we go wrong by not listening to all that Scripture has to say on a topic. These examples remind us of the need to be careful not to draw applications from Scripture that violate the harmony of Scripture – as happens all too easily in preaching.

Some Specific Issues

Scripture and missions

Think of a preacher who bases his sermon on this text:

> After this the Lord appointed seventy-two others and sent them two by two ahead of him to every town and place where he was about to go. He told them … "Go! I am sending you out like lambs among wolves. Do not take a purse or bag or sandals." (Luke 10:1–4)

Suppose the preacher proceeds to say, "Jesus tells his disciples who were going on a mission to carry no purse, no bag and no sandals. A principle we can draw out is that when we go on a mission trip, we should not take money with us; God will provide."

You might be quick to remember what Jesus said to his disciples on a later date:

> Jesus asked them, "When I sent you without purse, bag or sandals, did you lack anything?"
> "Nothing," they answered.
> He said to them, "But now if you have a purse, take it, and also a bag; and if you don't have a sword, sell your cloak and buy one." (Luke 22:35–36)

Your mind would be unsettled, and rightly so. This preacher would be drawing from one passage a principle that is clearly not in harmony with another passage. He is turning "what happened" into "what must happen", the descriptive into the prescriptive, in a way that violates the principle of the harmony of Scripture.

The preacher could say, "A principle we can draw from Luke 10:1–4 is that *sometimes* when we are on a mission it may be God's will that we do not have money with us." This principle would not contradict Luke 22:35–36 and would not violate the harmony of Scripture.

Seek the whole counsel of Scripture so that you do not make applications or draw principles that violate the harmony of Scripture.

Scripture and healing

Sometimes people come up with principles or teachings that they hang on to even when their lives are at stake. Regrettably, these principles do not always take the whole counsel of God into account and they can lead people astray, sometimes with tragic consequences.

Many years ago one of my colleagues, who was a brother in the Lord, came to my office. He looked very disturbed, and so I asked him what was wrong. His child was gravely ill. I asked if he had taken the child to hospital, and he said, "No. I don't believe in using medicine. I believe God can heal directly."

My response was, "That is true. God can heal directly, miraculously. The question is, will he heal in this particular way in this particular case? God works in various ways, God provides in various ways, God heals in various ways, but he does so as he chooses."

I implored my brother to take his gravely ill son to the hospital. I quoted many verses as I tried to show him that we do not know how God will choose to heal. For example, I reminded him of this verse:

> Oh, the depth of the riches of the wisdom and knowledge of God! How unsearchable his judgments, and his paths beyond tracing out! "Who has known the mind of the Lord? Or who has been his counsellor?" (Rom 11:33–34)

And of this one:

> As the heavens are higher than the earth, so are my ways
> higher than your ways and my thoughts than your thoughts.
> (Isa 55:9)

My colleague was unmoved: "I believe that God will heal miraculously, without medicine."

I reminded him of Naaman, the commander of the army of Syria, who wanted the prophet Elisha to miraculously cure him of his leprosy (2 Kgs 5:9–12). When Elisha did not do this immediately, Naaman became angry, but later his servant persuaded him to do what Elisha told him to do:

> So he [Naaman] went down and dipped himself in the Jordan
> seven times, as the man of God had told him, and his flesh was
> restored and became clean like that of a young boy. (2 Kgs
> 5:14)

I pointed out that Naaman believed that God would heal him miraculously and thought that he knew how God would do it. "But God healed Naaman the way God chose to. God works in various ways. You can believe in him for healing; but how he heals is up to him!"

I implored my colleague to base his beliefs about how God works on the whole counsel of God, not just on isolated passages. I reminded him that although God miraculously provided manna as food for the children of Israel for the forty years while they were in the wilderness, it stopped as soon as they came to a habitable land where there was produce they could eat (Exod 16:35; Josh 5:11–12). God provided miraculously, but he also provided naturally. Whether he used manna from heaven or the produce of the land, it was God who provided and he did so in his way and in his time. It is good that the children of Israel did not presume that there would always be miraculous food or simply wait for it to arrive, but also used the natural food that God provided.

In the same way, we should use the resources God gives us when it comes to healing. God can heal in a miraculous way if he chooses, but he has also given us resources like doctors, nurses and hospitals to help heal us. God is always the one who heals, but sometimes he does it through miracles and sometimes through medicine.

Medicine and medical care are not of the devil; they come to us from God. Paul was clear about this when he told Timothy to use wine as medicine (1 Tim 5:23). In fact, one of Paul's travelling companions was a doctor, for Paul speaks of "our dear friend Luke, the doctor" (Col 4:14).

I explained all this to my brother, emphasizing that "what matters is that you put your faith in God, not in medicine or in doctors." He left my office without further comment.

Several days later I saw him looking terribly sad. I asked whether he had taken his son to hospital. "No, I would not," he said. "How is he now?" I asked. The brother answered very sadly, "My son died." What a tragedy!

Whatever beliefs, principles or teachings we hold, we should take into account all that Scripture has to say about a subject so that the applications we draw are in harmony with all of Scripture.

> Our beliefs, principles or teaching should take into account all that Scripture has to say about a subject if our applications are to be wholesome.

Scripture and prayer

A sister in the Lord once arrived at our weekly prayer meeting at church, sobbing and devastated. We quickly asked her what was wrong. "My brother has died!" she cried. We knew about this sister's brother. He had been in hospital, and we had been praying for him.

She told us that she had gone out on a limb for God and told her family and relatives that God would do a miracle and raise her brother from the dead, hoping that this would help them believe the gospel. Alas! Despite her fervent prayers, her brother did not rise from the dead. She was devastated and embarrassed.

Her story is a clear illustration of the problems that can arise in relation to prayer and how God answers it. Many have been disillusioned because they have chosen to believe their interpretation of individual verses without taking the whole counsel of Scripture into account. When we consider all that the Bible has to say about prayer, we see that God answers prayer with a "yes", "no", or "wait".

Sometimes, God answers our prayers with a "yes" right away. This is what happened in Acts 4:23–31. Peter and John had been arrested by the Jewish authorities, and before they were released from jail they were "commanded ... not to speak or teach at all in the name of Jesus." The authorities threatened them with further punishment if they did not keep quiet (Acts 4:18–21).

Peter and John then went and told their friends about the threats and they prayed together. One of their requests was specifically, "Lord, consider their threats and enable your servants to speak your word with great boldness" (Acts 4:29). God answered, "Yes!" "After they prayed, the place where they were meeting was shaken. And they were all filled with the Holy Spirit and spoke the word of God boldly" (Acts 4:31).

But sometimes God answers prayer with a "no". This was his response to Paul's prayer in 2 Corinthians 12:8–9. Paul says that "in order to keep me from becoming conceited, I was given a thorn in my flesh, a messenger of Satan, to torment me" (2 Cor 12:7). He prayed fervently about this problem, but God refused to remove it. He answered, "No". He told Paul, "My grace is sufficient for you, for my power is made perfect in weakness" (2 Cor 12:9).

I had a similar experience a number of years ago when I wanted to leave the ministry and find another job. Times were hard and caring for my family was a daily and very, very difficult struggle. With my education it should have been easy to find a job and be relatively better off. I applied for many jobs and I prayed fervently. My friends got jobs easily. I did not. It was only years later that I came to understand that I had been trying to run away from God's calling on my life. No matter how hard I prayed, the Lord said "No".

Sometimes God answers prayer with "Yes, but not yet – wait". Abraham's case comes quickly to mind. When he was still called Abram, he prayed to God for a son to be his heir:

> Abram said, "You have given me no children; so a servant in
> my household will be my heir."

> Then the word of the LORD came to him: "This man will
> not be your heir, but a son coming from your own body will
> be your heir." (Gen 15:3–4)

God's answer to Abraham's prayer was "Yes, but wait", and Abraham had to wait many years. The waiting was not easy. Sarah thought that God's answer would be fulfilled through Hagar. She gave her to Abraham, and Hagar bore him a son, Ishmael, born when Abraham was eighty-six years old (Gen 16:15–16).

But Ishmael was not God's answer to prayer. About thirteen years after Ishmael was born, God reiterated his promise to Abraham, saying,

> "As for Sarai your wife, you are no longer to call her Sarai; her
> name will be Sarah. I will bless her and will surely give you a
> son by her. I will bless her so that she will be the mother of
> nations; kings of peoples will come from her."
>
> Abraham fell facedown; he laughed and said to himself,
> "Will a son be born to a man a hundred years old? Will Sarah
> bear a child at the age of ninety?" (Gen 17:15–17)

As you can imagine, the waiting was long and trying. But fourteen years after Ishmael's birth, Sarah did indeed bear him a son (Gen 21:1–5).

Like Abraham, we too sometimes find that God answers our prayers with a "Yes, but wait".

What attitude should we have then when we pray? Ultimately and fundamentally, we must be willing to say, "Not my will, O Lord, but your will be done!" whether God's will is "yes" or "no" or "yes, but wait". Jesus modelled this attitude in Gethsemane, where in great anguish he prayed to his Father saying, "My Father, if it is possible, may this cup be taken from me. Yet not as I will, but as you will" (Matt 26:39).

This attitude requires that we come to God with humility. A favourite verse for many people is 1 Peter 5:7: "Cast all your anxiety on him because he cares for you." However, we need to also read the sentence just before this one because that is where the need for humility is pointed out. In a more literal translation, the passage actually reads, "Therefore humble yourselves under the mighty hand of God, ... casting all your anxiety on Him, because He cares for you" (1 Pet 5:6 NASB).

One day, I was aghast to listen to an advertisement on the radio by a pastor who was urging people to come to his church so that he could pray for them. This pastor announced who he was and proudly added, "My nickname is 'the one who never fails in prayer'. Come with any burden and I will pray for you."

Where is the humility in these words? And who is the one taking the glory? Not only did this pastor lack humility, but he wrongfully implied that God's answer to prayer should always be "Yes". May God have mercy on us!

Remember that the principles you draw from a passage for application should take into account the whole counsel of Scripture. Also be careful not to turn "what happened" in Scripture into "what must happen" without considering other passages on the subject. Then you will hold wholesome beliefs and teachings and make applications in accordance with the principle that Scripture is in harmony with Scripture.

12

CONCLUSION

Many years ago when I was in high school, Idi Amin overthrew the government of Uganda in a military coup. Various groups in Uganda sent him congratulatory messages and students in our school started agitating that we should do the same. It became a hot issue and we gathered as a body to make a decision.

It looked as if those who wanted to send the message were going to win until a student named Etyang stood up and shouted, "Students in Nigeria never sent messages when the army took over their country. Why should we?" A student named Lawrence retorted, "How do you know they didn't?" Etyang shot back, "How do you know they did?" With that, the matter was settled, simply by the force of Etyang's voice. No message was sent.

There is something to learn here that applies to the preachers and teachers of the word today. Some preachers are full of energy and are great orators. When they speak you do not want them to stop. This is good. There is nothing wrong with speaking well.

However, there is a danger when preachers take over your mind by the force of their personality or oratory. I hope that this book will have made you alert so that you listen carefully to see whether what the preacher says is not only impressive externally but also reflects his applying the correct principles when it comes to the interpretation and application of God's word. We must not allow our minds to be taken captive by a preacher's reputation or personality or by the warmth and force of his or her voice.

We must scrutinize every passage of Scripture in its context, make sure that any interpretation is in harmony with the whole of Scripture, not turn "what happened" in Scripture into "what must happen" without considering other passages on the subject, and must apply Scripture appropriately. When we can do this, we will be treating the word of God with the respect it deserves, and each of us will be "a worker who does not need to be ashamed and who correctly handles the word of truth" (2 Tim 2:15).

NOTES

[1] Ralph P. Martin, "Approaches to New Testament Exegesis," in *New Testament Interpretation: Essays on Principles and Methods* (ed. I. Howard Marshall, Exeter, England: Paternoster, 1977), 221.

[2] Ibid.

[3] Joachim Jeremias, for example, bases his interpretation of Jesus' parables on the question, "What effect must His words have had on His hearers?" (Joachim Jeremias, *Rediscovering the Parables* [New York: Charles Scribner's Sons, 1966], 15). This question can also be phrased as "How would Jesus' Jewish audience have understood this parable?" (George Eldon Ladd, *The New Testament and Criticism* [Grand Rapids: Eerdmans, 1967], 180). By contrast, Gordon Fee and Douglas Stuart look at both what the recipients understood and what the author intended (Gordon D. Fee and Douglas Stuart, *How to Read the Bible For All Its Worth: A Guide to Understanding the Bible* [3rd ed.; Grand Rapids: Zondervan, 2003], 21–23).

[4] Ladd, 180.

[5] This issue is slightly more complicated when it comes to the Scriptures because of the combination of divine and human authorship. Theologians speak of the *sensus plenior*, that is, the deeper meaning intended by the divine author of which the human author was ignorant. We will not be able to deal with this issue in great depth in this book. For further reading, consult Raymond E. Brown, "The History and Development of the Theory of Sensus Plenior," *Catholic Biblical Quarterly* 15 (1953): 141–62.

[6] Paul seems to use this method at times, for example in Galatians 4:24–31. During Paul's time, the allegorical method was commonly used by Greek philosophers to explain philosophical matters and by Jewish rabbis to explain what the Old Testament said about God. However, whereas the Jewish rabbis had to rely on their imagination and creativity, Paul was inspired. He was not just another Jewish rabbi grappling with the deeper meanings of Scripture – he was writing inspired Scripture! And the divine author himself gave the deeper meanings to the Scriptures that Paul wrote. This is similar to how Caiaphas the high priest did not realize that he had prophesied Jesus' death, but the Apostle John interpreted the deeper meaning in Caiaphas' statement (John 11:49–52 – discussed in chapter 3). As ordinary interpreters, the critical point to note is that where there is a deeper meaning or referent, Scripture itself is the guide. Scripture interprets Scripture.

[7] Quoted from C. H. Dodd, *The Parables of the Kingdom* (London: Nisbet, 1961), 1–2.

[8] See Stephen Neill and Tom Wright, *The Interpretation of the New Testament 1861–1986* (2d ed.; Oxford: Oxford University Press, 1988), 1–34. This statement is innocently echoed by many an evangelical teacher of the Bible. However, to the proponents of the historical-critical method, the statement means that the Bible has nothing special about it, and inspiration and inerrancy are out of the question.

[9] John Knox and Gerald R. Cragg, *Matthew, Mark* (vol. 7 of *The Interpreter's Bible*, ed. George A. Buttrick; New York: Abingdon, 1951), 256.

[10] John Knox and Gerald R. Cragg, *Philippians, Colossians, Thessalonians, Timothy, Titus, Philemon, Hebrews* (vol. 11 of *The Interpreter's Bible*, ed. George A. Buttrick; New York: Abingdon, 1951), 405.

[11] I will not discuss the various kinds of literary genre in this book. However, it is important to be aware that the Bible includes genres such as poetry and history as well as letters, stories (like the parables), and theological arguments. Verses should be interpreted according to the genre of the passage. I recommend J. Robertson McQuilkin's book *Understanding and Applying the Bible: An Introduction to Hermeneutics* (Chicago: Moody, 1983) for further reading.

[12] Howard G. and William D. Hendricks, *Living by the Book* (Chicago: Moody, 1991), 214.

APPENDICES

APPENDIX 1

INTERPRETING WISDOM LITERATURE

A friend and I were listening to a preacher whose manner of speaking my friend found very strange. Just before completing a sentence, the preacher would pause and repeat a word or two. Sometimes the pause would come right in the middle of a word. His speech went something like this:

> I will not do – [pause] do it!

> I take this seri – [pause] seriously!

My friend said, "This preacher is stammering!" "No, he's not," I replied. "He is a Luhya, and that is the way the Luhya people show empha – [pause] emphasis!" My friend got the point. In the first example the preacher was stressing that he would never, ever do it. In the second, he was saying that he took the matter absolutely seriously.

All languages have some unique ways of saying things that interpreters need to be aware of in order to understand what is being said. This is also true of certain types of writing. For example, the wisdom literature in the Bible uses a particular style that we need to be aware of when doing interpretation. This style is called parallelism. We find it particularly in books like Job, Proverbs, Ecclesiastes and Psalms.

There are three different types of parallelism: synonymous parallelism, antithetical parallelism and synthetic parallelism.

In *synonymous parallelism*, the same thing is said twice. The second statement simply repeats the first using different words. Consider Psalm 114:1:

> When Israel came out of Egypt, the house of Jacob from a
> people of foreign tongue.

This type of repetition is helpful because the second phrase sheds light on the meaning of the first phrase, and vice versa. We can use this to clarify the meaning of ambiguous statements. Look at the example above. Some people might think that "Israel" was the name of an individual. The repetition of the same thought using the words "the house of Jacob" helps to sort out that Israel is not an individual but is the entire nation of the children of Israel, who came out of Egypt.

Sometimes the repetition is used for emphasis, as in Psalm 22:16:

> Dogs surround me, a pack of villains encircles me.

"Dogs" here is a synonym for a "pack of villains". The synonymous parallelism both explains who the dogs are and underscores the psalmist's contempt for these people.

In *antithetical parallelism*, the second idea is the opposite of the first. Read Proverb 12:16, for example:

> Fools show their annoyance at once, but the prudent overlook
> an insult.

The contrast between the first and second idea helps us to see exactly what the writer is contrasting. People who are foolish "show their annoyance at once". This behaviour is contrasted with that of people who are prudent or wise. The contrast is not that such people show their annoyance later, but that they "overlook an insult" entirely.

In *synthetic parallelism*, the second idea does not just repeat what has been said in different words, it also gives additional information. Psalm 11:4 is one example:

> The Lord is in his holy temple; the Lord is on his heavenly throne.

Here, the second part of the verse tells us that God's holy temple is also his throne. This knowledge will help you interpret a verse like Habakkuk 2:20:

> The Lord is in his holy temple; let all the earth be silent before him.

Because God's temple is also his throne, the whole earth should stand in awe and submission before the One who reigns.

There is one other point we need to note about the wisdom literature. Some have taken the sayings in books like Proverbs as promises. Then they blame God when they do not apply in their situation. For example, a woman once complained to me, "My son has grown up and no longer fears God at all. Yet I did everything I could to bring him up in the fear of the Lord, and Proverbs 22:6 promises, 'Train a child in the way he should go and when he is old he will not turn from it.'"

I asked her, "Did you do that?"

She replied, "Do what?"

"Did you actually train that child in such a way that he caught the training in his childhood?"

"Ours is a Christian home, and that is where he grew up," she said. Her very general words of defence left me wondering whether the boy had really been trained in the fear of the Lord. But that is not the point here. What is at issue is whether a proverb is actually a promise. It may help us to remember that a proverb can be defined as "a short, poignant nugget of truth, typically practical, and often concerned with the consequences of a course of behaviour".[12] "Nuggets of truth" are not promises. They are simply statements that certain types of behaviour will generally produce certain consequences.

APPENDIX 2

INTERPRETING FIGURES OF SPEECH

Many years ago, the whole of Uganda was gripped with fear of armed robbers who stripped people of all their wealth. Those who were fortunate escaped with their lives.

In those days, a father was accompanying his children to school at the start of a new term. He met a colleague and stopped to introduce his children, saying: "These are the robbers you hear me talking about!" A bystander whipped his head round to see the robbers! But the friend answered, "I know. I have also just paid the school fees, and now I am penniless." He recognized that the father was using a figure of speech and did not mean his words to be taken literally.

A figure of speech involves using words in an unusual way to paint a mental picture and communicate a point dramatically and effectively. All human languages use figures of speech, and the Bible is full of them.

Every figure of speech involves an element of comparison or association, and it is very important to identify what exactly this element is. For example, when the father referred to his children as "robbers", the relevant point of comparison was both robbers and his children take his money – but the children take it when he pays their school fees. In calling them "robbers", he was not implying that they were violent murderers like the robbers people feared. We should not make a figure of speech "walk on all fours", trying to find meaning in every detail.

Context is the key that will help you identify the point of a figure of speech.

It may be worth our while to look at a few kinds of figures of speech.

Simile

A simile compares one thing to another using the words "like" or "as". The Bible contains many similes, such as this one in 1 Peter 1:24:

> All people are like grass.

In what way are people like grass? What is the point of comparison? The context should help. When we read on, it says,

> All people are like grass, and all their glory is like the flowers of the field; the grass withers and the flowers fall, but the word of the Lord endures forever. (1 Pet 1:24–25)

Did you observe the word "but" in the last clause? It introduces a contrast: the word of God lasts forever; the grass lasts for just a little while. So, in the figure of speech, people are like grass because our lives are short. That is the point of the simile. There is no need to dig for other meanings by dragging up such issues as grass being used for grazing or weaving baskets.

Metaphor

A metaphor is like a simile that does not use the word "like" or "as". Instead the comparison is implicit. The father used a metaphor when he referred to his children as robbers. A very familiar metaphor is found in Psalm 23:1:

> The Lord is my shepherd.

This could be written as a simile "The Lord is like my shepherd", but the psalmist left out the word "like". Despite this, we still recognize that he is saying that the Lord is like a shepherd because he cares for us.

Sometimes our judgment of whether something is a metaphor can have important consequences. In the history of the church, many believers have lost their lives over the interpretation of Jesus' words in Matthew 26:26:

> Take and eat; this is my body.

What do you think? Is he using a figure of speech – a metaphor? Or does he want us to take his words literally and accept that the bread of Holy Communion has literally become his body?

Sometimes only one part of a metaphor is mentioned. We are given the image, but are not told exactly what it is being compared to. We have to infer this from the context. This is what the psalmist does in Psalm 22:16:

> Dogs surround me.

He does not say who or what these "dogs" are. We can, however, guess from the context. The rest of the verse reads:

> Dogs surround me; a pack of villains encircles me.

The evil men whom he refers to as "a pack of villains" are like dogs moving in to attack someone. The words help us to feel his fear as we shudder at the picture in our minds of what it would be like to be attacked by scavenging dogs.

There is another example of this use of metaphor in the story of the Canaanite woman who approached Jesus to heal her sick daughter. Jesus replied to her request by saying,

> It is not right to take the children's bread and toss it to their dogs. (Matt 15:26)

The verse does not say who or what is being compared to dogs, but from the context we can infer that it was the Canaanite woman or Gentiles in general. This raises an unsettling thought in our minds: "Did Jesus really call the woman a dog, just as the Jews used to call Gentiles dogs?"

Before answering this question, let us look at another contemporary example. A certain politician represented a community that was very reserved and did not normally comment on issues or express their views strongly. Some of his opponents came to the community, threatened the people and made them speak out. Commenting on the fact that people who were usually reserved were suddenly speaking out, the politician quoted a local proverb:

> A toad does not leave its hole in the daytime unless something
> is after it.

His opponents seized on this remark and told the community that the politician had called them toads. Defending himself, the politician said, "You have missed the point. The proverb is simply saying that toads come out because something is forcing them out. It means that things happen for a reason. When I quoted it, I was not calling the people toads!"

Jesus is using language in the same way that politician did. What point of comparison did he have in mind when he used this figure of speech? The Canaanite woman was a Gentile, and as such she was an outsider to the blessings that properly belonged to the children of Israel. This was the point Jesus was making. The woman understood him perfectly, and promptly replied,

> Even the dogs eat the crumbs that fall from their master's
> table. (Matt 15:27)

She was not calling herself a dog, was she?

Metonymy

Metonymy is a figure of speech that draws on associations, rather than comparisons. Rather than referring to something directly, it uses another word that is closely associated with it. There are several kinds of metonymy.

- *Cause for effect*: The cause is stated, but the effect is intended.

  > At the mouth of two witnesses, or three witnesses, shall he that
  > is worthy of death be put to death. (Deut 17:6 KJV)

Here the cause is "the mouth" which speaks, but what is actually being referred to is what that mouth says, that is, the spoken testimony of the witnesses. This is why the TNIV translates the first part of this verse as "on the testimony of two or three witnesses".

To take another example, God says,

  > I will pour out their own wickedness on them. (Jer 14:16
  > NASB)

Here the cause of what is happening is the people's wickedness. What is being poured out on them is the punishment for this wickedness. Once again, the TNIV translation hides this metonymy with its translation, "I will pour out on them the calamity they deserve." It gives the same meaning, but without using the figure of speech.

- *Effect for cause*: Here the effect is stated, but what the writer is speaking about is the cause of that effect.

  > I love you, Lord, my strength. (Ps 18:1)

Here the effect is "strength", but what the writer is referring to is the Lord who gives the strength.

- *The whole for the part:* The word used refers to some larger thing associated with the subject.

> For the grave cannot praise you. (Isa 38:18)

Here the subject is "the grave", but what the speaker is actually referring to is the dead people buried in the grave. Similarly, Isaiah says,

> The glory of the Lord shall be revealed, and all flesh shall see
> it together. (Isa 40:5 NKJV)

The broad meaning of "all flesh" is "every living thing", but the point that Isaiah is making is that every human being will see God's glory. Failure to recognise this figure of speech led one preacher to make a very startling interpretation of what Jesus meant when he told his disciples to "preach the gospel to every creature" (Mark 16:15 NKJV). Jesus meant that they were to preach to all people; he was not telling them to preach to animals.

- *The part for the whole:* An attribute or circumstance associated with the subject is mentioned instead of the subject itself.

> If harm comes to him on the journey you are taking, you
> will bring my grey head down to the grave in sorrow. (Gen
> 42:38)

Jacob refers to his "grey head", but what he means is that he will die and his whole body will be buried.

When God promised to bring the Israelites into "a land flowing with milk and honey" (Exod 3:8), he did not mean that they would have only those two foods to eat. What he meant was that they would have abundant supplies of luxury foods. The same principle applies when we say the lines from the Lord's Prayer:

> Give us today our daily bread. (Matt 6:11)

"Daily bread" represents the wider meaning "basic food". Bread is a luxury in some parts of the world, but in the region where Jesus lived, it was the everyday food of the poor, just as rice or cassava would be in other parts of the world. Knowing this historical information helps us to avoid praying for the wrong things.

Hyperbole

Hyperbole involves using exaggeration for the sake of emphasis. This is what the spies were doing when they reported back about the land of the Canaanites:

> The cities are great and fortified up to heaven. (Deut 1:28 NKJV)

When I first read these words as a boy, I was blown away by the idea of walls so tall that they reached heaven! I could not comprehend it! I did not recognize that this was an example of hyperbole, and so I misinterpreted the meaning. All that the spies meant was that the cities had very high walls.

APPENDIX 3

RESOURCES FOR INTERPRETATION

I am sometimes asked what resources people should get to help them to interpret the Bible correctly. Here are some of the basic types of books I recommend.

Bibles

The first resource for interpretation is, of course, the Bible. As you know, there are many translations of the Bible, and all translations involve interpretation of the meaning of the original Greek and Hebrew. All translations also strive for accuracy and clarity, but some clarify and interpret to such an extent that the structure of the original text is no longer visible. Look, for example, at how various English translations handle Numbers 6:6–7 (italics added):

> All the days that he separates himself to the Lord he shall not go near a dead body. He shall not make himself unclean even for his father or his mother, for his brother or his sister, when they die, because *his separation to God is on his head* (NKJV).

> Throughout the period of their dedication to the Lord, the
> Nazirite must not go near a dead body. Even if their own
> father or mother or brother or sister dies, they must not make
> themselves ceremonially unclean on account of them, because
> *the symbol of their dedication to God is on their head* (TNIV).

> *His hair is the sign of his dedication to God*, and so he must
> not defile himself by going near a corpse, not even that of his
> father or mother or sister (Good News Bible, TEV).

The NKJV closely follows the structure and flow of the words in the
original Hebrew text, but the English feels rather wooden. The TNIV
irons out some of the difficulties in interpreting the original text and
presents a translation that is more interpretive and clearer than the NKJV.
The Good News Bible takes the freest approach to interpreting and
explaining the original Scriptures.

It is easier to recognise issues of interpretation if you use a version
that has tried to preserve more of the structure and flow of the words in
the original text. Here are some versions I recommend:

- New American Standard Bible (NASB)
- New English Translation (NET)
- New King James Version (NKJV)
- Revised Standard Version (RSV)
- New International Version (NIV)

It can be a good idea to own several different versions of the Bible.
Then whenever you want to interpret a verse or passage from Scripture,
you can compare various versions. Doing this will alert you to issues of
interpretation. To show you what I mean, let's look at Romans 1:17.
This is how the Good News Bible (TEV) translates it:

> For the gospel reveals how God puts people right with himself:
> it is through faith from beginning to end. As the Scripture
> says, "The person who is put right with God through faith
> shall live."

When you read this translation, you think that Romans 1:17 is perfectly clear and that there are no problems when it comes to interpreting it. But when you start to look at other versions, you will begin to note some possible problems.

> For in the gospel the righteousness of God is revealed – a righteousness that is by faith from first to last, just as it is written: "The righteous will live by faith" (TNIV).

> For in it the righteousness of God is revealed from faith to faith; as it is written, "The just shall live by faith" (NKJV).

The more literal translations like the NKJV include phrases such as "the righteousness of God". Does this refer to God's being righteous, or the righteousness he gives to us? And what does "from faith to faith" mean? Is it referring to growth in faith?

To be able to answer these kinds of questions, you will have to do some research. A helpful way to begin is to look up any cross-references in your Bible to help you find passages that use similar terms or deal with a similar subject. You can then compare the passages and see whether they throw light on the question you are asking.

If you can, get a Study Bible with maps, book outlines, cross-references, a concordance and brief notes that explain difficult terms and give background information. These features will help you interpret what you read. There are many Study Bibles out there, but a few that I would recommend are:

- *Zondervan NIV Study Bible*
- *Zondervan TNIV Study Bible*
- *ESV Study Bible*
- *Ryrie Study Bible*

Concordances

A concordance lists all the words used in the Bible alphabetically and includes a brief quotation from every verse where each word is used. This tool can be used to help you find a verse when you can only remember the words but not where it is located. For example, if you had forgotten which psalm contained the words, "The Lord is my shepherd", you could look up "shepherd" in the concordance. One of the entries under that heading would be "Ps 23:1 –The Lord is my *s.*" You would immediately know where to find the rest of the psalm. This feature can also be useful when you want to check the context of a verse that someone quotes without telling you where it comes from.

You can also use a concordance to do word studies, looking at how the word is used in different parts of Scripture. Suppose, for example, that you want to try to resolve the ambiguity we identified in the phrase "the righteousness of God" in Romans 1:17. It might be helpful to know where else this phrase occurs in the New Testament. If you look up "righteousness" in a concordance, you will find that the exact phrase "righteousness of God" occurs eleven times in the New Testament. It is used in Matthew 6:33 and James 1:20, eight times in Romans, and again in 2 Corinthians 5:21. What do these statistics tell us? They tell us that nine of the eleven occurrences of this phrase in the New Testament are in Paul's letters. This topic was obviously very important to Paul and is a key concern in his letter to the Christians in Rome.

Similarly, if you wanted to think about how marriage is treated in the Bible, one place to begin would be by looking up all references to the words "wife", "husband" and "married". You would find many examples of good and bad marriages and much information about how God sees marriage.

Academic concordances like *Young's Analytical Concordance to the Bible* or Strong's *Exhaustive Concordance of the Bible* will give you much information about the original Hebrew or Greek words used. Such concordances tend to be expensive and can be difficult for those who do not know these languages. If you want to use one, you can probably find one in a Bible college library near you.

For most people, the limited concordance at the back of a Study Bible will be sufficient. If you want something more, but not a full academic concordance, you could consider buying something like the *NIV Handy Concordance* (Grand Rapids: Zondervan, 1990). Note that reference to the NIV in the title. All concordances refer to the words used in a particular version of the Bible. Many of the older ones are based on the KJV. While these are still helpful, they may not have words that are translated differently in a modern translation.

Bible Dictionaries and Encyclopedias

Bible dictionaries and encyclopedias are helpful resources because they give the following types of information:

- Definitions of words and terms
- Background information on events, names, places, personalities, symbols, and the social life of Bible times
- Maps, charts and illustrations to help you picture everyday life in Bible times
- Overviews and background to the books of the Bible
- Articles on relevant topics

Let's use John 4 to illustrate how to use a Bible dictionary. The Samaritan woman Jesus met at the well has this to say:

> "You are a Jew and I am a Samaritan woman. How can you ask me for a drink?" (For Jews do not associate with Samaritans.) (John 4:9)

Who were the Samaritans? Why was there such animosity between them and the Jews? You can find the answers by reading the article on the Samaritans in a Bible dictionary.

Later, the Samaritan woman says:

> I can see that you are a prophet. Our ancestors worshipped on this mountain, but you Jews claim that the place where we must worship is in Jerusalem. (John 4:19–20)

What mountain was she talking about? You will find the answer to that question too in a Bible dictionary article about the Samaritans.

Here are some dictionaries I can recommend:

- *New International Bible Dictionary*

- *NIV Compact Dictionary of the Bible*
- *The New Bible Dictionary*

Bible Commentaries

When you use a commentary, you are consulting others who have spent time studying and researching in order to be able to interpret the Bible. But don't just assume that these writers must be right because they are scholars. You should expect them to be able to back up their conclusions using solid principles of interpretation.

You can access many commentaries in Bible college and seminary libraries, and you can find good, easy-to-read commentaries on Web sites such as www.BibleGateway.com or Wycliffe's www.easyenglish. info. If you are able to purchase commentaries to build your personal library, the following one- or two-volume commentaries are affordable and cover the whole Bible.

- *Africa Bible Commentary* (Nairobi: WordAlive / Grand Rapids: Zondervan, 2006).
- *Bible Knowledge Commentary* (Colorado Springs: Cook, 2002).
- *IVP Bible Background Commentary: New Testament* (Downers Grove, Ill.: InterVarsity Press, 1993).
- *IVP Bible Background Commentary: Old Testament* (Downers Grove, Ill.: InterVarsity Press, 2000).
- *New Bible Commentary* (Downers Grove, Ill.: InterVarsity Press, 1994).

The one-volume *Africa Bible Commentary* is being supplemented by commentaries on individual books of the Bible. This series is being published by HippoBooks as the Africa Bible Commentary Series. You can get more information about these books and other helpful books from publishers such as Africa Christian Textbooks (ACTS) in Nigeria (www.africachristiantextbooks.com), Step in Ghana (www.stepbooks. org) and WordAlive Publishers (www.wordalivepublishers.org) in Nairobi.

FURTHER READING

- Duvall, J. Scott and J. Daniel Hays *Grasping God's Word: A Hands-On Approach to Reading, Interpreting, and Applying the Bible* (2nd ed.; Grand Rapids: Zondervan, 2005).
- Fee, Gordon D. and Douglas Stuart, *How to Read the Bible for All Its Worth* (3rd ed.; Grand Rapids: Zondervan, 2003).
- Hendricks, Howard G. and William D. Hendricks, *Living by the Book* (Chicago: Moody, 1993).
- McQuilkin, J. Robertson, *Understanding and Applying the Bible* (Chicago: Moody, 1992).

www.ingramcontent.com/pod-product-compliance
Lightning Source LLC
LaVergne TN
LVHW030634080426
835508LV00023B/3365